Kashpar

Center for Basque Studies
Basque Diaspora Series, No. 8

Kashpar

The Saga of the Basque Immigrants to North America

Joseph Eiguren "Kashpar"

Center for Basque Studies
University of Nevada, Reno

N

Generous financial support for the publication of this book has been provided by the Basque Government

Basque Diaspora Series, No. 8
Series editor: Xabier Irujo

Center for Basque Studies
University of Nevada, Reno
Reno, NV 89557
basque.unr.edu

Book design: Kimberly Dagget
Cover design: Daniel Montero
Cover photos courtesy of Eiguren family. See pages 28 and 78 for
    captions to photos used for illustrations

Library of Congress Cataloging-in-Publication Data

Eiguren, Joseph.
Kashpar : the saga of the Basque immigrants to North America / Joseph Eiguren (Kashpar)
    pages cm. -- (Diaspora and migration studies ; no. 8)
        ISBN 978-1-935709-51-0 (paperback)
    1. Eiguren, Joseph. 2. Eiguren, Joseph--Family. 3. Basque Ameri-
cans--Biography. 4. Immigrants--United States--Biography. 5. Sol-
diers--United States--Biography. 6. World War, 1939-1945--Personal
narratives, American. 7. Jordan Valley (Or.)--Biography. 8. Boise
(Idaho)--Biography. I. Title.

E184.B15E54 2014
305.89'92073--dc23
2014007416

Contents

Introduction by Xabier Irujo   1

Preface   5

1. Early Recollections   7

2. A Little Schooling   15

3. Life in the Basque Country   25

4. Decisions   37

5. Travel to America   43

6. A New Beginning   53

7. Encounter with the Trapper   59

8. A Lonely Life   65

9. Small Incidents at the Sheep Camp   73

10. A Sheepherder's Fear and Other Changes   77

11. Farewell Party   81

12. Life in the Army   85

13. Engagement   93

14. My Marriage to Aurora   103

15. N.C.O. Training   111

16. Departure   123

17. Assignment to the 79th Division   129

18. Fear of Never Returning   135

19. Spectacular Breakthrough   141

20. The Needed Rest that Did Not Come   147

21. Experience in Belgium   157

22. Ambush in Pussey   163

23. Entertainment on the Front Line 167

24. Vosges Mountains Attack 171

25. Rest After 137 Days of Combat 175

26. Return to the Front Line 179

27. Advance to the Siegfried Line 185

28. First Strong Point of the Siegfried Line 189

29. Hospital Incident in Strasbourg 193

30. Return Home 199

31. My Recovery 203

32. Life in My Beloved Idaho 209

Epilogue

At the urging of our sons,
Alfred J. and Roy L. Eiguren,
I have dedicated this book to
our grandchildren
Amaya and Joseph

Introduction

Joe Eiguren, "Kashpar," was raised in the Basque Country during very difficult times. These were the times of the dictatorship of King Alfonso XIII. Joe felt strongly about the Basque cause so, when he came to the United States in 1934, that was very much part of his life and he played a role in the fight against fascism and totalitarianism by serving in the American army in WWII.

Over time he became very interested in Basque politics and Francisco Franco's continued dictatorship in the Basque Country. His son Roy recalls that Joe was particularly upset and concerned with the support that the American government under President Eisenhower gave Franco beginning in 1953 and continuing for some time. Back in the late 1960s he approached members of Euzkaldunak Inc., the Boise Basque Center, to see if they would express their political concerns about the U.S. support of Franco. Their answer was that "Basque clubs don't get involved in politics." But when dealing with the Basques, everything is politics. In general, when dealing with the survival of the cultural heritage of a nation, everything becomes politics. Indeed, speaking in Basque in the Basque Country from 1937 to 1975 was considered a political offence by the authorities of the Francoist regime. It was "against the law." This is why Joe organized classes of Basque in the Basque Center but even that was initially resisted by the Basques in Boise who have learnt at Spanish schools "that to speak in Basque was punishable." But ultimately they allowed Joe to teach. And Basque language classes are currently taught to hundreds of students every year in Boise and Boise has even known the creation of a Basque preschool.

Joe became acquainted with Pete Cenarrusa through his son Roy when the last went to work for Pete in the summer of 1970 as a clerk in his office in the summers. Roy introduced his father to Cenarrusa in 1970 and they became quite close. That was the time when Cenarrusa actually became very concerned about what we call "the Basque conflict." In 1973 Joe met Pat Bieter, the organizer of the first trips to learn Basque to the Basque Country (an illegal and dangerous activity at the time, in the Basque Country.) Bieter was a faculty member at Boise State University and he conceived the idea. Joe was asked by Pat if he would go and be a part of the initial group of faculty members, and that's how that came to be. That way Joe became the part of the group of faculty members of the Boise State University abroad study program in Oñati.

That was really the first opportunity Joe had to go back to the Basque Country after he had left when he was nineteen years of age in 1934. He was—his son Roy remembers this vividly—deeply offended, deeply impacted by the fact that the Franco regime still existed in 1973-74. The Guardia Civil was the armed branch of a highly repressive machinery. He and his students, many of whom live in Boise today, remember that very clearly. The road blocks, the searches, all these men wearing machine guns and the impacting "tricornios." That there was still a dictatorship in Western Europe in the mid 1970s, a regime with no constitution, no parliament, no political parties, no elections since 1936. It just seemed unfathomable.

When they returned from Oñati Joe Eiguren and Pat Bieter became very active in opposing the Spanish government and they developed, collectively, a stronger relationship with Pete Cenarrusa. As we can deduce from the sequence of events beginning in 1970, the three of them became very active in promoting the end of Franco's dictatorship and the beginning of a transition to democracy in the Basque Country by collaborating with the U.S. Congress and U.S. Senate and also with members of the Basque government in exile. Their efforts led to a number of meetings from 1970 on with Senator Frank Church and eventually resulted in the establishment of a new organization known as *Anaiak Danok*. Justo Sarria became the president and

Julian Atxabal, Teodoro Totorikaguena, and Mari Carmen Egurrola among others, became part of the organization. The group
raised money and became active in the fight for democracy and
human rights in the Basque Country.

Many of the members of *Anaiak Danok* were trying to find
ways to advocate for the Basque cause, to support Basque freedom, and Basque independence. Joe, who had a natural interest
in writing, though never formally educated, loved to write when
he found something of interest to him. That was how he began
writing *Kashpar* and press articles. Joe was very knowledgeable
about Basque history, the Basque language, and Basque politics
as well as a terrific storyteller. Pete Cenarrusa, the great politi-
cian that he was, chose to use the political process. The three of
them, with Pat Bieter, contacted members of the Idahoan sen-
atorial delegation where they got support along with Senator
Laxalt to put pressure on the Spanish government.

That was the time of the generation of the first Basque
immigrants who were so fluent in the Basque language and had
undergone the political and socioeconomic crisis provoked by
a long lasting dictatorship. This was the very beginning of the
Oinkari dancers which started in the late 1960s. In terms of promoting Basque culture, Basque history and the Basque language,
Joe Eiguren was a leader in the Boise Basque community.

This book is the story of Joe Eiguren, an average Basque
immigrant to the United States, who came seeking a new life
when the Basque Country was devastated by the political terror
exerted from the Spanish government before and after 1936 and
the subsequent economic depression.

Xabier Irujo

Preface

As the reader of this narrative, if you are expecting to find a literary work in it I would like to tell you not to read it—you would be disappointed and wasting your time. Also, if you have the illusion that it may be diverting in your leisure time, expecting to find something fantastic and novelesque, again, I discourage you from reading it.

I am not a writer and I do not pretend to be one. I grew up in Euzkadi (Basque Country) speaking Basque, although clandestinely, for the speaking of it was prohibited. I learned Spanish by compulsion; the Spanish authorities rammed it down our throats. I learned English by necessity after I emigrated to America. I have never attended any school here and I learned to speak, read, and write English on my own. Therefore, my writing is not fancy because I do not know how to enhance my phrases with the elegance of great writers. If I would try to do it, the result would be ridiculous.

I only wish to relate a simple story of plain people, not just mine, as it is the same story of those who were confronted with similar problems when they emigrated to this country. So, speaking in the first person through me, I am in reality telling you the story of thousands of my ancestors, Basque immigrants, who emigrated to the U.S.A. years before, and after, I arrived here.

Joseph Eiguren (Kashpar)

1

Early Recollections

My first recollection as a very young child was the sound of hammering in the stairway in the house in which we lived in Lekeitio in the Basque Country. It was a dreary October night. I was in the kitchen, alone, which was dimly lit with a single, small light bulb hanging from the ceiling. My brothers and sister must have been in their rooms. The rain was pounding furiously on the red clay, tiled roof. The rattling of the dry leaves falling from the trees, together with the sobbing of my mother in one of the adjoining bedrooms, was very frightening to me. I knew instinctively that something tragic had happened, but I did not know what, as I was too young to realize it.

Suddenly the hammering ceased, only to be replaced with the sound of sharp, heavy footsteps. It sounded like a platoon of soldiers marching in unison with heavy hiking boots, or like a group of men carrying the statue of a saint in a procession as they often do in the Basque Country on festive occasions. In reality, it was a procession, a very sinister procession at that. The footsteps that I heard were those of the six men of the municipal street cleaners who were carrying the body of my father who had died earlier that afternoon, a victim of the 1918 epidemic known as the Spanish Influenza. He had died about 4:00 o'clock in the afternoon, and by 10:00 o'clock that evening he was placed and nailed in the casket, carried to the cemetery by these men, and buried.

As the sound of the men's wooden shoes, or clogs, diminished, my Mother's crying increased.

Joseph Eiguren, Kashpar, as a one-year-old, a few days before boarding the ship to cross the Atlantic, in 1916

Suddenly, everything was quiet, at least for me. I do not remember what took place after that. Did I fall asleep? Did my

"Amuma" (that is, my Grandma) or someone else take me away? I don't remember seeing anybody around. All I remember is that that incident is very vivid in my mind, even to this day. It left an indelible mark on my mind. I was only three years old when this incident occurred. Too young to realize the enormity of the loss that my Father's death represented to our family. With his death we were affected not only with the grief and pain that tragedies of this magnitude inevitably cause, but also with the difficult economic conditions that befall a family. The modest resources that our Father was able to accumulate in his short life (he was only 38 at his death) would soon be gone. From then on, it was a continuous struggle for us to survive.

My parents came to the U.S. singly from the Basque Country in the early 1900's. They were some of the early Basque settlers in a small town named Jordan Valley, located in eastern Oregon in the foothills of the majestic Owyhee Mountains. Although they knew each other in the Basque Country, their relationship was nothing more than that of two friends. Their courtship originated in Jordan Valley, and as a result they were married in Nampa, Idaho in 1908. There were four children out of this union, of which I was the youngest; my sister Pilar the oldest; three brothers—Luis, Domingo (Txomin), and me, respectively.

My Father, who was known as Kashpar which was the name of the ancestral dwelling where he was born at the foot of the Pyrenees Mountains overlooking the turbulent waters of the Bay of Biscay and the uniquely picturesque Cantabric Coast, was a farmer as a young man. He was one of several brothers and sisters, five in all, including himself. Their farm was much too small to support them all; therefore he decided to emigrate to America to seek his fortune. Because of his lack of skill, compounded by a lack of English, he, like most Basques that emigrated to the U.S., engaged in herding sheep.

Kashpar parents, Domingo (Kashpar) and Maria, on their wedding day Nampa, Idaho.

In a few years of working with sheep he accumulated some money, and, putting his savings with another compatriot, a boyhood friend, they formed a partnership; both started their own sheep-raising business. In about two years, his partner decided that he wanted to return to the Basque Country, so my Father bought his partner's interest and continued in business several years longer by himself. In a relatively short time he made it fairly good, financially. He would have liked to continue in this business longer, but my Mother, who suffered from chronic bronchitis, wanted to return to the Basque Country. So, in spite of his success in the livestock business he decided to return to the Basque Country to comply with my Mother's wishes. I was scarcely a year old when our family returned to their native land and I was told by my mother that I learned to walk on the ship as we crossed the Atlantic. Two years later, in 1918, my Father died.

In his haste to go back to the Basque Country my father did not take the time to dispose of his business in the U.S. He entrusted virtually all of his business to one of his closest friends—about 1600 head of sheep, several horses, all the necessary equipment to operate a sheep business, and the house the family owned in Jordan Valley where I was born.

At his death the business he left in the U.S., as well as the cash he took with him which he had invested in property and stocks, was irrevocably lost, leaving my mother completely destitute to raise four children (ranging from eight to three years old).

I recall a few incidents concerning my father, in addition to the one surrounded his untimely death and burial. I remember a few of them. I was playing in the kitchen of our house, down on all fours. I bumped against the leg of the kitchen table and started to cry. My father, who was sitting and talking to my mother, picked me up and pampered me. I don't remember what he said to me, but I do remember that he used some sort of baby talk, yet I can't remember the sound of his voice.

Another time, I was playing in front of our house with my sister Pilar, and I spotted him coming home from one of the orchards he owned. I tore loose from my sister's hand and ran to meet him. I have a vivid picture of how he looked. He was tall and slim with a very thick moustache, and he had his coat thrown loosely over one shoulder. He picked me up and put me on his shoulders with my feet astraddle of his neck, and I steadied myself by clasping my hands under his chin. It seems strange that I have such vivid memories of these incidents of my father since I was so young, but then the memories fade away.

Our sister Pilar, the oldest of our family, at age twelve.

One year later, exactly on the first anniversary of my Father's death, my brother, Luis, died of pneumonia. Although I was a year older at his death than I was at the time of my father's, I have a better recollection of my father's death than I have of my brother, Luis'. Luis was almost eight years old at the time of his death. He contracted measles. As he was getting over them, he suffered a relapse, which, compounded with pneumonia, resulted in his death.

Scarcely three years later tragedy struck our home again, this time with the death of our sister, Pilar. I remember her well. I was almost six years old when she died; a victim of spinal meningitis at the age of 12. I have a very distinct memory of her sickness and her untimely death. Pilar was a very pretty girl with a round face, long black curly hair and a pair of big, black, saucer-like eyes. She, being the oldest, and I the youngest, were very close. My recollection of Pilar's sickness, was one day when I went home from school for lunch, I could hear her crying and yelling in unendurable pain. I started to eat the lunch that my mother had fixed for me. I was standing up. I tried to eat, but I couldn't. My mother was sobbing in an adjoining room and Pilar, from her deathbed, was crying and asking God, "Dear God, heal me or kill me, please remove these pains from me." I burst out crying and left the house. My next recollection of her was when I returned home. I don't remember whether it was the same day or a few days later, but it was in the evening; everything was quiet. Pilar was quiet for a change. Mother, Amuma, a few neighbor ladies and the priest, Father Goikolea, who was also a family friend, were in Pilar's room. Perhaps they were reciting the rosary. I do remember that I was happy to see Pilar not crying in pain as I had seen her do for so long, and to me that was an indication that she was better.

Soon Amuma said, "Koxetxu" (that means Little Joe in Basque), "Get ready, for it is time for us to go home." On occasions such as this I usually stayed with my Amuma; I was her pet. As we were about to leave Father Goikolea called me to Pilar's bedroom where they all were and told me to kiss my sister goodbye. I was too small to reach her, so he picked me up so that I could kiss her. I can always remember how pretty she looked with her round, pretty face. She looked so peaceful and tranquil, in contrast to the times she had been in agony and begging for death. She did not open her eyes nor utter a sound as I kissed her goodbye. I was sure that poor Pilar was fine. With that, Amuma and I left for her home in Zubieta, which was about a mile from where we lived.

The following morning, right after I got up, I asked Amuma, "How's Pilar?"

"She is fine," she replied. "She's asleep. Go and see her," she said.

I did after breakfast. When I got to our home, Pilar was in a different room. During the night she had been moved to a room that was usually reserved for guests. I was happy to see her in that state; no pain, no agony. Within two or three blocks from the house, as I left to go towards the center of town, I noticed a man carrying a white casket. I stopped in my tracks and watched him go in the direction of our house. As I suspected, he went to our house with the casket. Then I knew the casket was for Pilar. I burst out crying. I realized that Pilar was dead. I didn't remember whether I went home to see her or whether I went to find my playmates in town. Pilar, too, was gone.

My mother was left a widow with four children ranging from eight years (the oldest) to three years (the youngest). During the next three years she lost the two oldest children. Of the two surviving sons, Txomin, the oldest, left for America at the age of sixteen, and I left at nineteen.

2
A Little Schooling

I don't remember how old I was when I started school. It was a private school, and the classes were conducted in Basque. The teacher, a Basque lady, was a very strict disciplinarian. If she loved anything more than her charges, the little Basque boys and girls, it was the Basque language and culture. Not only did she teach in Basque, even though the speaking of Basque was prohibited by the Spanish authorities, she also prepared her students to continue the struggle for its preservation. As a wise old lady, she knew that as long as the Basques were under the Spanish yoke, the fight for freedom would continue. But unaware of problems of this type, I left the private school and enrolled in a public school. Most of my friends were attending public schools, and I wanted to join them.

The public schools were conducted in Spanish, and the teachers were exclusively Spaniards. I don't remember having learned anything constructive in the public schools. Most of the teacher's time was devoted to expounding the glories of Spain during her grandeur in the discovery, conquest, and early colonization of the New World. The little Basque students, all boys, about 50 or more in one room ranging from 8 to 15 years, spent their time listening to our teacher's diatribes in Spanish (which we didn't understand) or learning patriotic Spanish songs. The learning of these songs was compulsory, and strangely enough I remember only part of one of them. Not because I was impressed with the song, but because of the beating I took for singing it (with certain innovations that I learned from some of the older boys). I would like to tell you in Spanish how it goes and give you a translation:

> "Soldado soy de Espana, estoy en el cuartel,
> contento y orgulloso por haber estado en él."

Literally translated, it means:

> "I am a Spanish soldier, and I am in the barracks,
> I am very proud to be one of them."

Our version, that is the older kids', went like this:

> "Soldado soy de España, estoy en el cuartel, recogiendo las colillas que tira el coronel."

Which means:

> "I am a Spanish soldier, and I am at the barracks picking up the cigarette butts thrown away by the Colonel."

It rhymed perfectly. I sang this particular version just as loud as I possibly could one day towards dismissal time when the teacher, whose name was typically Spanish, Leonides Martínez de Torres, a mousey little guy—pale face with eyes like a little rat, said in Spanish, "Who was that?" Everybody in the school was quiet. When he asked the question, you could hear the proverbial pin drop. He asked again, but nobody was "squealing" on me. That made him mad.

He said, "Until I find out who was singing that song, the whole class will remain here."

Finally, someone said, "It was Kashpar."

That was me. I'm sure whoever squealed on me was the son of a Guardia Civil or a Carabinero, who were all Spaniards. "Come here," he commanded.

I knew what was coming. I went to the front of his desk, scared to death. He ordered me to kneel down; then hold out my hands with the palms up. He placed several books on each hand for me to hold. This was the accepted method of punishment. Rendering me helpless, he hit me right across my mouth with his fist and knocked me down, bleeding through my nose. He picked up a stick, which was at least an inch in diameter and about four feet long, and he literally broke it on my back, and I *literally* wet my pants. The books flew all over the place. I tried to get away from the....., but I couldn't. Finally, by struggling, pushing, kicking and shoving, I managed to get away from him and ran to the door. At the door, I looked back and yelled at him, "You pig, hit your mother," and gave him the equivalent of the American "obscene gesture" in Basque. I ran out and never returned again. I was 11 years old.

The next day, I went out at the usual time just as if I was going to school, but I never did. In the afternoon, the same thing. For three, maybe four months, I followed this pattern. Sometimes my friends played hooky and when we got together we went to a little hill that was called the Calvary. There was a cave in this hill where anthropologists sometimes would dig. We would wonder what they were doing and sometimes watch them pull human skulls and bones out. Later we found out that these bones were over 60,000 years old. During the time that I was not in school, I also passed the time going to church as an altar boy. I helped serve Mass, sang in the choir, sometimes I sang Requiem solo at the funerals and helped ring the bells in the bell tower of the church, which was a beautiful basilica built in 1380. One particular time, when five or six of us kids were doing some work in the church cleaning it and putting some kind of dope on the candles of the chandeliers to make them easier to light for the big festivities, we swiped a few bottles of wine used in celebrating Mass, and bought several packages of cheap tobacco, and went to the cave in the Calvary hill. We got drunk on the wine and sick smoking the cheap tobacco. When we came back to town late that afternoon, we were really worried we might be caught. We were afraid to go home. In my case, my mother might smell tobacco or wine or both, so we went to a public fountain and washed out our mouths and then smelled the breath of each other, asking, "Can you smell me?"

Finally, after all this time, the question of school came up. Mother found out that I hadn't been going to school. I was afraid I might get another beating, but I didn't. I told her what had happened, why I quit school, and all about the situation. In a few days she arranged for me to go to another private school. There were only six students in this school. The teacher was a Catholic priest by the name of Father Eguzkiza. He was a well-known orator who used to go all over the Basque Country, giving talks and sermons. I remember hearing some of his sermons in church. There was a demand for him all over the Basque Country. He was a strong Basque patriot who, incidentally, was jailed by Franco during the Civil War. I went to this school until one month before my 13th birthday.

Father Eguzkiza taught me many things that were not in the school curriculum. For example, some of the things this teacher taught me, were: when in a strange or foreign country, never ask a taxi driver, "Do you know where such-and-such a place is?" Say, "Take me to this address." By saying it firmly, you will convince the taxi driver that you know exactly where the place is, and he will take you directly to the address you gave him. Another thing I learned from him was that if you happened to be in a foreign country, be sure that you learn to say, "How much?" when making a purchase. Even if you are not familiar with the language or the money exchange, the seller doesn't know, so he or she will tell you the right amount. Not knowing the amount I gave a dollar.

They gave me change. Another minor item he taught me was how to steal chickens at night without the chickens making any noise. The method is to find an opening like a window, push a stick through it until you reach the chicken's perch, tap their feet, and they will instinctively leave the perch and climb onto the stick. You slowly retrieve the stick. When the chicken reaches you without a noise, you twist its neck, "click," like that.

I did have the opportunity to make use of the first two "hints," like the taxi bit and the asking "how much" even though I couldn't count the money, but I never had the need to apply the third bit of knowledge, yet. But who knows what will happen? I hope that our economic condition improves before it comes to that!

Kashpar and his brother Domingo (Txomin) –left–
in the Basque Country ca. 1922.

Our financial situation was very bad after my father passed away. We did have a reasonably good house in which to live and plenty to eat. I always suspected that our Grandma made sure that we were all taken care of in this respect. I wanted to quit school and go to work. I wasn't doing too well towards the last of my schooling. I didn't even attempt to study. I was a poor student.

When a student didn't know his lessons, Father Eguzkiza didn't dismiss the student too quickly; he had a way of making him learn his assignment. After school he would go by his house, which was six stories high, and have students like me who wouldn't study at home wait by his door on the front steps until we learned the lesson. Almost every day I would learn my lessons by his door. I learned them quickly that way. I would ring the doorbell, he would come out, and I would recite the lesson and answer his questions. I did really well that way.

One day he came out and said, "If you can learn your lessons so quickly here, why don't you do it where you are supposed to, at home before you come to school, or when you have time for a study period at school? This means that you can do it. From now on, don't ever ring my doorbell. When I am ready, I will come out."

The idea behind having the student by the teacher's door was to shame the student. A lot of people would come by and naturally they would think (or at least we students would imagine that they would think), "Here is a stupid boy who can't learn his lessons." To avoid these people I learned my lessons as fast as I could to get out of there, but the teacher was smart and knew what I was doing, and so he said, "Don't ever call me; I will get to you when I am ready."

After that I didn't learn my lessons anywhere, even by his door. The last couple of months that I went to school with this teacher, we didn't get along too well.

The climax of my getting out of that school was odd. Our town was full of pigeons, so many that they were a nuisance. The mayor of the town issued an order that anyone who wanted to get a pigeon could do so. Not with guns in the city limits, but with slingshots. Practically every kid in town made a slingshot. We didn't have any radios at the time; the town crier, a man who came with a drum, usually issued the order. In every plaza and every square in town he would stop and beat on that drum several times. There is a certain way that he would beat it to give a routine announcement, and another way he would beat it if he was issuing the mayor's order or proclamation. He issued the mayor's order all over the town regarding pigeons, and everybody started making their slingshots to shoot the pigeons. Within a few days, there was practically not a window or a light bulb in public places intact in that city. In view of this destruction the order was rescinded after a couple of days. It was also announced that anybody found in possession of a slingshot would be prosecuted. I had a really nice slingshot made for the purpose of shooting pigeons, and I just couldn't bring myself to destroy it. I went to school one day with the slingshot under my shirt. While I was waiting to get into school, I was tempted to shoot it. I got out a pocketful of little rocks we used to shoot the pigeons with, and took aim at the church bell. I hit it and it made a lot of noise— more so than what I expected.

Kashpar and his brother Domingo (Txomin) -right
in the Basque Country ca. 1926.

Kashpar as a student in the Basque Country before migrating to the Americas.

The priest who lived near the church, heard it. He must have known right away who it was. He came to school and had us stand up in front of him. He looked at me and said, "What do you have under your shirt?" "Nothing," I said. "Nothing? Well, how come your shirt is so bulgy? Come here!" I went to him, he pulled my shirt up, and there it was. The slingshot! He examined it and said, "You did a good job on this."

He kidded me a little bit, then took a little knife out of his pocket and cut the rubber and leather parts of the slingshot into pieces and then gave the handle back to me. He never hit or beat us like the Spanish teachers did, but one way he punished us was by pinching our arms. My arms, the right one especially, used to be black and blue with his pinching. Also, there was one knuckle he would use to hit us over the head.

He told me, "You know, you don't respect anybody, you don't respect your teacher, you don't respect your mother, you don't even respect the city mayor. What are we going to do with you?" Then he went into my lessons, my behavior, my not learning, and finally he said, "I want to talk to your mother. We are going to straighten this out once and for all."

He did talk to my mother that afternoon, and the next morning when I went to school, he gave me a choice. "Do you want to study?" he asked me. "You do have the capabilities to study, but with your attitude you are not going to, and your going to school is not going to do you any good unless you take a different attitude. What's bothering you?"   I replied, "I just want to go to work. I want to go to work and make some money. This is not for me."

"In that case, there is no point in your continuing in school," he said. "If that is your wish, then that is mine also."

So I was kicked out of school. The following day I started to work building fishing boats in a small shipyard, working with 24 grown men. I was the only young kid, not quite 13 years old, among the 25 of us. I worked at the shipyard for six years until I came to the U.S.

3
Life in the Basque Country

The next six years were difficult for me. The working hours were long and the wages were very low, equivalent to the American 5£ per day, six days a week, from 8:00 a.m. until dark.

Primitive working methods were used due to the lack of mechanical devices and the lack of electricity in our jobs. Often the whole crew would go out to the mountains to cut timber: oak, eucalyptus, pine, cypress, and other trees used in the building of fishing boats. Everything had to be sawed by hand, often right in the mountains, as there were no adequate means to transport the large trees to the shop. I was one of many who engaged in this type of work in the Basque Country before coming to America. Others were Baserriterrak, that is, farmers. They were dedicated to farming, but upon coming to America began herding sheep for want of something better.

Others (who for generations dedicated themselves to fishing until coming to America) became sheepherders, in contrast to their previous occupations. The fisherman's life was colorful, but rugged and dangerous. Not very profitable. A crew of fishermen consisted of a "patroia," that is the skipper; an engineer, who mans the engine; the fireman, who keeps the boiler going and keeps the steam up; about eight other regular fishermen; and a young boy who did the cleanup and kept the boat in shape.

Each crew had a "Dei Egitekua," literally a caller. These are the women whose function was to raise the crew in the morning, if and when the weather permitted the fishermen to go to sea. Each crew had a place, the headquarters, where they transacted all their business. Invariably, this place was a tavern, and the distribution of their earnings took place there. On a typical day the town weatherman (usually a seasoned, experienced, older fisherman, assigned to this position by certain local authorities), went out to the most salient spot in the village about 2:00 or 3:00 a.m. and scanned the horizon. He would forecast the weather and determine if the fishermen should go out or not. If he predicted good weather, then he notified the women (callers) who were waiting for his forecast. If he said go, the women went out to wake up their respective crews. There was something fascinating about this waking of the men. These women had magnificent voices, although perhaps uncultivated, but really something worth hearing. They called "Joxe Inaxio" (Spanish—Jose Ignacio), "In the name of God, arise!" In the dark, misty, rainy morning, their powerful shrill voices sounded so unreal that one shivered, getting goose bumps. After her job was done, the caller went home to her children or to church with the rest of the fishermen. Her husband was one of the fishermen. The men would rise quickly, pick up their fishing gear, and go to the church, except for the fireman and the boy. These two go straight to their boat. The fireman to raise the steam of the boat and the youngster to do little chores before departure.

Every morning around 4:00 a.m., on the days when fishermen went out to sea, a special Mass was celebrated for their safe return. The departure was spectacular; literally hundreds of men came out of the Basilica in absolute silence, without a word to one another, their wooden shoes pounding on the cobblestone streets on their way to the waiting boats, compounding with the sound of the scores of boilers building up the steam prior to their departure, vibrating the otherwise quiet, sleepy village. The men took their positions on the boats, and one by one the boats started out to the open sea in an orderly manner, one boat after the other, separated by only a few yards. A mile or so out to sea, they would disperse in all directions and within a few minutes would disappear in the distant horizon. Their eyes are fixed on the land. On top of the highest mountain that surrounds the village was the "talayero," the observer. His job was to spot schools of fish (mostly sardines, anchovies, or tuna), and notify the fishermen out in the sea of his findings. As strange as it may sound, this was accomplished by using the primitive method of smoke signals. In this way, he informed the fishermen of the location of a school of fish, the latitude, the longitude, the approximate distance from the land, and the direction it was traveling.

Once the skipper of the fishing boat gets the signal from the talayero or observer, he goes full speed ahead, chasing the school of fish. Five or six boats or more may go after the same school of fish. The first boat that reaches the school lays the nets and catches the fish, but any other boat that comes near it and the catch is not completely aboard, the skippers of the arriving boats yell "partners" and they all share in the catch. It was an unwritten law that they abide by.

At the end of the season it takes them several days to settle their accounts because of large numbers of partnerships, not only between the fishermen of the same town, but also with the fishermen of the neighboring villages as well.

The farmers' lifestyle was different from that of fishermen. My maternal grandparents were farmers and lived in Zubieta which was the name of the farm, and there they raised thirteen children of which my mother was the oldest. I spent a lot of time with them in my youth in this ancestral home and remember well the kind of life they led which will depict the life of an average Basque farmer.

Their house was a two-story, stucco structure. The ground floor consisted of an entry way, a kitchen in the front half of the house and the barn in the second half, or the back end of the house. The second story was the living quarters such as the living room and the bedrooms. A stairway in the entry way led the way to the second floor. The kitchen with a dirt floor was equipped with a sink (no running water); a fireplace where Amuma, that is grandmother in Basque, did all the cooking—no stove!—for her large family; a cupboard full of dishes; a long table with a bench against the wall on one side and some chairs on the other side. Considering the conditions, the house was kept immaculately clean.

Zubieta's ancestral dwelling of my maternal grandparents.

Atxitxa got up each morning at 5 a.m. and attended the daily, first mass. After returning from church, he would have his light breakfast and then would go to the field to cut some fresh grass for the cows (2 of them), feed the hay to them and milk them. While he performed his tasks, the rest of the family would get up and in a sort of "everybody for himself fashion each took care of themselves. The girls stayed home and the boys went to their jobs. All of them were working in the three local shipyards.

The noon meal was impressive. At the time, I rather took it for granted, but now looking back in retrospect I appreciate how beautiful and meaningful it was. Each member of the family had their own place to sit around the big, long table. Atxitxa would come in, open the two windows in the wall that separated the kitchen from the barn where the cows were lowing in anticipation of the food they were about to receive from Atxitxa who, with incredible dexterity, sliced the beets with a sickle and fed the cows. Then he would wash his hands and sit down at the head of the table, remove his txapela (beret), as did everybody else, and say the grace which began with the sign of the cross, give the blessing, and ended with the first half of the Lord's prayer: Aita gurea, our Father, etc., and the second half: Emonegizu gaur geure eguneroko ogia (give us our daily bread, etc.) by the rest of the members of the family. Then Atxitxa would take a big loaf of bread, perhaps a foot in circumference, in his left arm and with a butcher knife in his right hand would carve a cross in the bread. He then proceeded to slice it and pass it to each member of the family. Amuma would then bring big platters of succulent food that she had prepared in an open fireplace during the morning. To me, this scenario was the closest thing resembling the Last Supper—the shape of the table, the seating arrangement, everything looked so much like it. I often think of Atxitxa and the family when in church even today when I hear the words of the Communion Service, "I am the vine and you are the branches. Without me you can do nothing." These words remind me of Atxitxa and Amuma too, Atxitxa slicing or breaking the bread and distributing it among the members of the family in a true sense of absolute communion.

After the noon meal, Atxitxa read the newspaper, took a short nap and then went back to work in his fields. Amuma went after the dishes. She did not read the newspaper, not because she did not have the time, but because she couldn't read it. She did not know how to speak, read or write Spanish. She knew only Basque, but even in Basque she could only speak it. She could not read nor write Basque because of the brutal suppression by the Spanish government's absolute monarchy. Since the use of Basque language was prohibited and was not taught in the schools, Amuma learned to speak it from her parents.

Atxitxa was an imposing figure, not only physically for he was six feet plus tall and weighed about 200 lbs., but he was a symbol of strength of character and a very compassionate man. Amuma was a very beautiful and intelligent lady, although illiterate. Of the thirteen children she bore, six emigrated to America.

This is a picture of Kashpar's maternal grandparents, Koshe Benantzio and Jakoba Nabarro and their thirteen children. The lady whose right hand is resting on the right shoulder of Atxitxa is my mother. The young man on the right of my mother is Pasko, described in chapter three.

Among these six was Pascual, better known as Pasko who came to this country at the age of thirteen and developed a livestock empire in Jordan Valley. Perhaps Uncle Pasko's way of thinking or philosophy would best describe Amuma's intellect. One day while I was visiting him on his ranch, we were discussing various subjects including the plight of the Basques in Euzkadi (Basque Country), and suddenly almost like changing the subject in the middle of the conversation he said, "You know, Kashpar, the Basques are like cameras." I couldn't figure out the parallel, so I asked him what was the similarity between the Basques and the camera.

"Kashpar," he said, "the camera captures everything you snap or take a picture of. It could be that it captures a parental love for their children or vice versa, a panorama, scenery, anything, but if these pictures are not developed nothing would come out. The same with the Basques, they have just as much as anybody else in their minds, but it has never been developed because of the cruel oppression of unjust "governments." What he said reminded me of Amuma and her intelligence that had never been developed. She was a beautiful, intelligent and compassionate lady. I loved her!

Whether a farmer or a fisherman, all got together on festive occasions and would participate with no distinction. All occasions started with a solemn Mass in the morning, usually at 10 o'clock. After the church services, a dance called Aurresku is performed in the village square and it is always presided over by the city mayor and the parish priest. This authentic and genuinely Basque ceremonial dance was described by Strabo, Hannibal's scribe. It is as old as the Basque race itself.

In the afternoon, there were always some big events: weight lifting, wood chopping, and jai alai game. Toward the latter part of the afternoon, the festivities culminated with a dance in the open in the village square. At sunset the church bells sounded the Angelus and everybody dispersed. The women and the girls would usually retire to their homes. Men and older boys would go to the taverns to discuss the day's events and perhaps play some cards.

As time went by, I became aware of many things. I realized the seriousness of the Basques' plight. I remember how the older men used to meet occasionally and clandestinely. They were known as the Bizkaitarrak, meaning literally the Biscayans, but the term was actually synonymous with the Basque Nationalism. I witnessed the closing of the Basque centers, the raiding of the Bizkaitarraks' meeting places, the confiscation of the Basque history and cultural books, the burning of them in public by the Spanish Civil Guards, and the jailing of some of the Bizkaitarrak. In view of all of this, it was not hard for me to decide to join them and actively and diligently work for the cause. I admired these men's quiet, serene courage—and the tenacity with which they fought their oppressors. I learned to love everything pertaining to Basque; the language spoken in spite of the fact that Basques were not allowed to speak it, their history, fables, songs, dances, music, everything. The Bizkaitarraks' efforts to regain their freedom paid off.

In 1931 the tyrannical dictator of Spain fell, and by the abdication of the king, Spain and all the peninsula became a republic. With the advent of the republic, many changes took place in the Basque Country; not only culturally, but socially, and in other aspects as well.

The Spanish new democratic government allowed the Basques to speak their native language, reopen their cultural centers, perform their ancient dances which they were not allowed to perform, display their flag, and to do whatever they wished to do to maintain and preserve their culture which they were not allowed to do so since 1839.

Among those activities were the opening of the Basque centers in the different towns. Almost every Sunday there was an inauguration or opening of a Basque center in some Basque town. On these occasions we, the boys and girls, would gather about 5:00 a.m. in the main church of our town to hear Mass, receive Communion, assemble in the city "plaza" and move on foot to whichever town the inauguration may be, waving our flags and singing our patriotic songs. Thousands of people gathered on these occasions from different towns.

About 3:00 p.m. we always met in the city's handball park or "Frontoya" to hear the leaders of the Basque freedom movement, i.e. Jose Antonio Aguirre, Telesforo Monzon, Esteban Urkiaga, and many others.

Urkiaga was better known by his pseudonym "Lauaxeta." He was a writer and a poet. He became a very close friend of the Spanish all-time great poet, Federico Garcia Lorca. Ironically both of them were assassinated by Franco. History books say "executed" as if they were criminals, but they were assassinated because of their fierce love for freedom.

In 1972 I wrote a little book and dedicated it to Urkiaga because I admired him so much when I was a youngster in Euzkadi. In 1974 I learned that his father and my paternal grandmother were brother and sister!

For the first time (1931) in the history of the Basques the "Bizkaitarrak" founded the first labor organization which in Basque was known as the "Euzko Langille Batza" or "The Solidarity of Basque Workers" and through it our working conditions, as well as salaries, improved.

Kashpar, siting, with his friends in the Basque Country. It was customary to take a picture before migrating.

"The solidarity of Basques workers" was exclusively a Basque labor union with no connection to the powerful Spanish "Union General de Trabajadores" = "General Union of Workers," of socialist inclinations, nor with the "Confederación Nacional del Trabajo" = "National Confederation of Workers," also leaning strongly to the left. On the contrary, it was blessed and endorsed by the Catholic Church. Among the many reforms brought about by this organization were; the legal determination of hourly rate and salaries, and ending the shameful feudalistic system of working from daylight to dark, six days a week for the equivalent of 50 American money. The workers were classified as helpers, apprentices, first and second class workers (in our case marine carpenters), and set the wages accordingly. The hours were set at eight hours a day, following the pattern of England, the U.S.A., and other more advanced nations. Another measure was to prohibit the employment of children under fourteen years of age and making it compulsory to attend school for those children.

When the time came to formally organize the union locally in Lekeitio, a meeting was convoked with the participation of hundreds of workers attending it to elect the officers. The election was held, but it was declared invalid. Although I was not a candidate for any office, I received scores of write-in votes for president of the local union.

Since I was only sixteen years old in 1931, the election was declared invalid as I couldn't vote or receive votes until I was eighteen! After the second round of elections, my uncle, the one that slapped me, was elected president.

To illustrate how life was for us under the tyrannical Spanish dictators, I would like to relate a little incident that occurred on one Christmas Eve during the Spanish oppression of the Basques. In the Basque Country, Christmas is the biggest day of the year. On this day, nobody works; even the bakers are off. However, the biggest and most important celebration in commemoration of the birth of Jesus is on Christmas Eve. On this day, all members of the family gather for the evening meal. Even those members of a family who might be away from home in colleges or working in other towns of the peninsula get together for this occasion that is celebrated with a special meal consisting of many delicacies; sea bream, snails, and other items that people may not usually eat during the year. It is what could be considered an annual family reunion. After dinner, everybody goes out visiting local taverns and singing Christmas carols in the streets until church services start at midnight. On this particular occasion, I was separated from my friends. We came out of a tavern, and I stopped in a public rest room between the tavern and the main plaza of the town. As I came out of the rest room singing Christmas carols in Basque, I was stopped by two Civil Guards. One of them put his rifle about a foot from my chest and told me, "Don't you know that you are not supposed to sing in Basque?" I tried to tell them something, and the one aiming his rifle at me said, "One word out of you, and I will let you have it." I did not know what he meant, whether he was going to shoot me, or hit me with the butt of his rifle, so I didn't say anything. After I joined my friends, they wanted to know what happened. There were a couple of other groups of young guys interested in knowing what happened. I explained to them, and we all decided to work the Civil Guards over. We dispersed in different directions, and first one group started to sing Christmas songs in Basque, and the Civil Guards started chasing them; then another group started to sing, and the guards chased them. We let the Guards come as close to us as we dared, and then ran as fast as we could while another group started to sing. For about two hours we had the Civil Guards running in circles all over the town until midnight, which was the time for us to go to Mass.

4
Decisions

As a very young boy I worked with my mother in a fish cannery during the summer. There were several canneries in town. That was the biggest industry—fishing and the related businesses, mostly fishing canneries and building fishing boats. In the summertime, when school was out, my mother and I worked in these canneries. The pay was low and the hours were incredibly bad. I say incredibly bad, because we had to go to work whenever the fish came in. Often the fishing boats came in loaded with anchovy, sardines, or tuna at midnight or maybe 2:00, 3:00, or 4:00 in the morning, and the fish had to be processed right away. People from the factory came to our house at these hours in the morning, asking us to come to work. I remember many times when I was a nine- or ten-year-old boy, getting up at one or two o'clock in the morning and going to these canneries to clean fish. The fish were kept in big tubs of salt water, and my job was to put them in the baskets and take them over to the tables to the ladies who did the cleaning. It was very hard work. My hands were always burned with salt water; and the place stunk to high heaven. We worked several hours and then again in the middle of the afternoon they might call us again to do the same job.

When I went to work building fishing boats, as I have said, I lacked one month of being 13; I didn't have to go to work in these fish canneries. I worked until I was 19, building the fishing boats. That was rough also. I was the only kid with 24 grown men, and when I started out my job was to pick up the tools, sharpen them, oil them and supply the men with tools and the other material they needed, including drinking water. They handled me pretty rough.

On one occasion, one of the guys got peeved at me for something, I didn't know what I had done wrong, but he was so disturbed that he kicked me right in the pit of my stomach, and completely knocked me out. I couldn't breathe. There was quite a deal about this. The other workers who witnessed this incident didn't like it, so they called this guy. I thought they were going to have a fight because of it.

Another time, while we were working in the port fixing boats, some workers were on the scaffold that was hanging from the boat, and I was in the boat giving them the things they needed. One of the men asked me for something, and I think I misunderstood him, or maybe I was distracted by the people who were watching us from the pier. In any event, I gave him the wrong tool, and he slapped me. I will never forget that. He was my uncle. He really slapped me hard, and I couldn't understand why. When I was about seventeen, again we were working in the seaport, and one of the fellows asked me for something. Again, as a young kid, I suppose, I was distracted by the people watching us work from the pier, and I did not give him what he asked for. He called me a bunch of names, and told me, "I am going to hit you so hard that you are going to see sparks flying from your face."

By that time, at seventeen, I was a pretty big kid, and pretty strong. I didn't like what he said, so I told him, "Why don't you try it? Come on, I am ready."

He backed off. He got real pale-faced, and never did come after me. The guy who slapped my face, my uncle, was proud of me for calling this guy's bluff. I wasn't bluffing, I was ready for him.

I mentioned what my duties were as a flunky. I usually did these chores on Sundays with no extra pay. The workers used the tools and dropped them anywhere. One time my boss gave me hell (reprimanded me as he so often did) regarding the tools. I thought I had enough of that and decided to quit. I picked up my coat and left the shop. The boss, a big, strong, solidly-built man of about 225 pounds, followed me outside of the shop and asked me: "Where are you going?"

"I am quitting," I answered.

"Why?"

"Because you always give me hell for something that I didn't do. You know that I take care of your tools. It is the other workers who use them and drop them anywhere. Yet you always reprimand me for the benefit of the others because you haven't got the guts to tell them off."

I was about to cry. He looked at me for a long time and said: "Joxetxu, you are right. Come on, follow me," he said and I did, just like a little pup. He climbed up the scaffold, called for the attention of the workers and really gave them hell. Things changed considerably after that. I was about 15 years old when this incident occurred.

These are just small things that happened during my growing up in the Basque Country. As I was approaching 19, I knew that I had to do something. Since I was an American citizen I had the opportunity to leave and come to the U.S. However, I felt that I belonged in the Basque Country. I had my friends, my mother, and my girlfriend. I didn't know what to do. Whatever I was going to do, I had to make up my mind before I was 21 if I wanted to retain my American citizenship. I hated to leave them all there with the conditions the way they were and the way we were living. The thing that really induced me into the decision to come to the U.S. was that I felt that I didn't want to be a Spanish citizen, and if I didn't come to the U.S. before I was 21, I would have forfeited my right to continue to be an American citizen.

It was not easy to make a decision. I was one of the few who had the opportunity to go to North America, but it meant leaving everything behind. Perhaps I would never see my friends and relatives again. Perhaps I would never return to the Basque Country. After considerable thought I decided to go to America and take my chances. One of the main factors in making this decision was that from America I could be of more help economically to my mother.

One sad day I bid farewell to my beloved land and began my journey to a strange, faraway land. The day of my departure has to be one of the most memorable days of my life; my mother's goodbye to her youngest and last child, knowing that she would never see him again, and my knowing that I would never see my mother again.

After a sleepless night, I got up early on the morning of September 17, 1934, the day of my departure to the unknown. I was very nervous, excited, and perhaps a little afraid, and in my excitement I forgot to place the safety part of the razor and shaved without it, nicking my face in several places. I doctored the cuts by rubbing them with aftershave lotion and patching them with pieces of Bamby cigarette paper to stop the bleeding. Mother and I were alone, but we hardly exchanged a word during the time I was getting ready to leave. Finally, when I was ready, I picked up my suitcase and a trench coat, and as I was heading toward the door, I called, "Mother, it is time for me to leave. I must go." She came to meet me at the door. I knew she had been crying. We said goodbye, and she put her arms around me and kissed me on both cheeks. She started to cry again. She opened the door for me.

"Good luck to you, Son; take care of yourself," she said almost inaudibly, as she was sobbing. I said goodbye to her and left, and from a distance I turned to look back towards our house and there she was, standing on the balcony watching me with a handkerchief in her hand. I put my suitcase down and waved to her. She waved back with her handkerchief. I picked up the suitcase and moved on out of her sight, never to see her again. It was one of the saddest moments of my life.

In a minute or two I arrived at the bus station, and all of my relatives and friends were there waiting for me. All of them noticed my nicked face. After a sad but effusive farewell, I clambered into the bus and left my hometown of Lekeitio.

My Uncle Patxi and Aunt Luisa Eiguren accompanied me as far as a town of Zornotza (in Spanish, Amorebieta). There they helped me board a train to Donostia (San Sebastian), and from there on I was heading towards the Pyrenees.

By mid-afternoon, the small, rattling train began climbing the Pyrenees and through a network of tunnels finally crossed the Pyrenees Mountains. We arrived in St. Juan de Luz, France after dark. There we had to change trains to continue without trip, and within a half an hour we were on our way to Paris.

After traveling all night, we arrived in Paris at 8:00 a.m. the following morning. When I started out to America, I did not know how long it would take to get to my destination, Boise, Idaho. The first big city on my journey was Paris, a magnificent city, but I was really concerned about the more pressing problems I was about to face than about admiring the wonders of Paris, like where would I spend the night, and was I going to be able to find the right train in this huge terminal that would take me to Le Havre the next day.

When I came out of the train in this huge terminal, I was completely lost. "Where will I go from here," I thought. The place was very crowded. People were on the move in all directions as if all of them, except me, knew where they were going. While I was there, confused, not knowing where to go or how to go, a middle-aged man in a black suit came to me. He was a tall, thin man with a dark complexion. He must have realized that I was lost, so he came to my rescue.

"Hello, young man," he said in Spanish.

"Hello there, sir," I replied.

"Where are you going?" he asked me.

"I am going to America."

"Yes, but where are you going from here?" he asked.

"I am going to Le Havre from here, and I am to take a ship, île-de-France, in Le Havre for America."

"What a coincidence," he said, "We, too, are going to Le Havre, and are to embark on the île-de-France on the 19th."

"Would you like to join us?"

"Yes, sir, I would." I was really happy to join them. He took me over to join his friends. He first introduced himself. His name was Jose Garcia Balbuena, a Spaniard. Then he introduced me to his companions, Mr. and Mrs. Manuel Ramos. Mr. Ramos was a Spaniard, and his wife was a Puerto Rican. There was one other Spaniard with them from the same town in Spain, Santander. This fourth fellow and the others didn't get along too well. They argued a lot. Of course, this is something I found out later. They argued because they did not agree in their political philosophy. I was very happy with Garcia Balbuena.

We took a taxi to the hotel, as all of us had arrangements at the same hotel through the travel agency. The difficulty for me would have been to find out where this hotel was. After we were settled in the hotel, they again hired a taxi and we went on a short tour around Paris. I do remember going to some department stores, and that was the first time that I had ever seen an escalator; I wasn't sure whether I was going to handle it. I remember distinctly going through the Arc de Triomphe, the Eiffel Tower, the Champ de Elysees, and some of the most interesting points of Paris. We retired at the hotel that night.

5
Travel to America

The following day, early in the morning, we went to the train terminal, boarded the train and started out to Le Havre. I didn't have any trouble since I was with these people. This was Jose Garcia Balbuena's 11th trip to Spain from America. It was an ordinary trip without any problems.

We arrived in Le Havre about 5:00 o'clock in the afternoon. There, too, the hotel arrangements were made. We spent the night in Le Havre. I noticed that Balbuena was able to speak French also. He was quite a man. He teased the French waitresses, and I know he fibbed a lot to them about me. I could tell from the look on their faces, looking at me, and asking me something in French.

The following morning we boarded the ship to come to America. The name of the ship was île-de-France, one of the biggest in the world at that time. There was only one bigger that hadn't been in operation as yet, and that was the Normandy.

On the île-de-France, they accommodated us in our cabins. The married people had their own cabin and the single people theirs, two people to a cabin (two men or two women, whatever the case might be). I was assigned to a cabin with this other Spaniard, who Balbuena didn't like very well, but he was a Spaniard, so it was lucky for me that I had someone to converse with. Balbuena saw to it that I was assigned to a table so that I ate with him and Mr. and Mrs. Ramos. There were four to a table in the dining room. It was a beautiful ship. I didn't know that they made ships that big. We had all our meals together, but I had difficulty in selecting from the menus as they were in English and in French, and I knew neither of the languages, but Balbuena helped me with that too, so I got along fine. The trip was very good. At the end of the evening meals, they usually cleared the dining room, and we always had a movie. After the movie, there was generally some spontaneous musician that gave us some sort of a concert, sometimes a pianist, sometimes a violinist. Then after the concert, they usually had a dance until midnight in the dining room, which was a large room.

On one of these nights, my friend Balbuena and I stayed for the dance, but we didn't dance. We just listened to the music and watched the people dance, and about 10:00 o'clock Balbuena said, "I am tired. I think I am going to bed, but you don't have to come with me. You can stay here and listen to the music and watch these people dance."

"O.K.," I said, so I stayed. About 11:00 o'clock, I decided to go to bed, too. While the dance was going on, I started out towards my cabin, right through the center of the dance hall where the people were dancing. When I got to about the center of the dance hall, there was a couple dancing and they stopped when I approached them. The man was all decked out in a fancy uniform. He was the chief of our compartment which was the tourist class, the cheapest. He, speaking in French, I suppose, wanted me to dance with the girl he was dancing with. By sign language he took hold of me and put us together, dancing. Over in Basque Country when we waltzed, we did it right-handed. This was the first time in my life that I danced left-handed and it was a disaster. My coordination was bad. I am sure that I stepped all over the girl's toes. I never forgot that, and I am sure that this girl never forgot it, either! At the end of the tune, I proceeded to my cabin.

Usually, after the dance, dinner, or movies, we gathered around our tables and visited and Balbuena would tell these girls a lot of stories about me. I didn't know what was going on. Later he tried to explain to me how he kidded these girls. Max Schmelling was on this ship and was coming to the U.S. to fight for the world heavyweight championship. Balbuena told these girls that

I was coming to the U.S. also for the same purpose—to fight Max Schmelling! The funny part of it was that the girls believed him.

Balbuena was a very energetic man, tall and thin, and very aggressive. He spoke good English, French, and Spanish. He told them just anything he wanted to, which was not the truth, and the girls believed him. For example, he told them that I fought Paulino Uzkudun and other well-known boxers of that time, and they believed him.

After 5-1/2 days of traveling on the ship, we arrived in New York. I remember that we stopped in a certain place, and learned later that it was Ellis Island. I also remember seeing the Statue of Liberty. It impressed me so as I had seen the pictures, but actually seeing it was something great! The immigration authorities separated the American-born citizens, like me, from the others, who were naturalized citizens, and immigrants. They took me, along with others, to a different room inside the ship to check my documents. I was separated from my friend, Balbuena, and others, for he was a naturalized citizen. When I came out of that room I was completely lost. I went to see where Balbuena and my friends were, but they had already gone to shore. I started out on my way and was going in the wrong direction. I came across one of the girls that we used to visit with during our travel. I suppose she was in her 30's, short, very pretty, small girl. She was traveling with two big suitcases, one in each hand, in the opposite direction from me. She smiled at me and stopped, put her suitcases down, and I think she tried to tell me that I was going in the wrong direction, but I did not understand her. I am sure that she was telling me that I was supposed to follow her or something like that. We were in the tourist class and I was heading towards the second class exit. She couldn't make me understand. Finally, she gave up. We shook hands and she said something to me. I suppose she said, "Good luck to you" or something to that effect. She picked up her suitcases, and smiling, left me, and I continued going on my way in the wrong direction.

Finally, I found the exit where the people were going out, and sure enough that was the second class instead of the tourist class. I thought, well, what difference does it make, if I have to go out, I might as well go wherever I found an opening to get out. I went out and nobody said anything. When I got on the plank ready to go down to the pier, I saw Balbuena waving at me. I think he suspected that I got lost in that big ship, and he was keeping an eye on all three exits. He took me over to his friends, and then he arranged for a taxi and saw to it that I was going to the right hotel. The Santa Lucia Hotel was where most of the Basque immigrants who came from the Basque Country stayed because this hotel's owner was a Basque fellow by the name of Valentin Aguirre, and he had connections with the travel agencies. Arrangements were made for me to stay in this hotel. Balbuena, who was a widower, had a girlfriend waiting for him at the pier. The three of us went to the Santa Lucia Hotel in New York City. While we were traveling toward the hotel, which was quite a long way from the pier where we disembarked, Balbuena asked me to stay in New York.

"Why do you want to go to the west?" Balbuena asked me.

"I have my relatives there, I also have a brother there, and I am committed to go to the west," I replied.

"In the west you aren't going to see anything but cows, sheep, and stuff like that. You speak very good Spanish. If you want to stay in New York, I will give you a place to stay. I am an electrician by trade. I can teach you my trade and see that you go to school at nights so you can learn English, because with your Spanish you will not have much trouble in learning English."

But I insisted on going to the west for the reasons that I have already stated—my brother, my relatives, and a lot of Basques in there. I said, "No, I have to go to the west."

He realized that I was determined to go to the west. When we arrived at the hotel, he took me in and we registered, and he said, "O.K., young man, if you must go west, go to the west, but one thing, if you are going to live in America, make sure that you learn to speak English. Go to school at nights or whatever, but be sure you learn to speak English, because it is a necessity in America."

I promised him that I would try my best. I told him that I didn't know how long I would be in the west. I might go back to the Basque Country, but if I decided to remain here, I promised that I would try to learn English.

We shook hands, he grabbed me and embraced me effusively, "Goodbye, young man, it has been a pleasure to know you."

"The same with me, and thank you very much for everything," I said, and he left. The Basques have a tendency to dislike or even hate the Spaniards merely because of the problems between us, but as for me it is not so. I do not consider all Spaniards to be anti-Basque. I do know that the Spaniards deprived the Basques of their freedom. It is true. But it is also true that the Spaniards at the advent of the Republic in April 1931 gave the Basques a certain measure of freedom. In other words, there are Spaniards who deprived the Basques of their rights and freedom, and there are Spaniards that granted the freedoms, benefits, and privileges to the Basques. In my case, I was practically lost when I arrived in Paris, and this man, Balbuena, a Spaniard, came to my rescue, knowing I was a Basque which made no difference to him, and he took me under his wing. It made no difference to me either. I was happy that he befriended me, and there are millions of Spaniards like him.

I remained in New York for two days, and left on the third day for Boise, Idaho. While in New York, the first night I was there, I just wanted to see a boxing match that was going to take place in Madison Square Garden between Tony Canzoneri and Barney Ross. Over in the Basque Country we read a lot about these boxers. We were avid fans of boxing. That was our favorite sport. Knowing that the match was going to take place that night, I thought that I wanted to see it, and somehow I found Madison Square Garden in New York. When I got there I didn't have the nerve to go in because I didn't know how much money I had, I didn't know how much the admission was going to cost, and I couldn't count American money. If it took just about all the money I had, I thought, what would I do the rest of the way from New York to Boise? So I just stayed there and watched people go in. Somehow I found my way back on my own to the hotel. As I was going to where the boxing was to take place, I had made a mental note of some of the great big skyscrapers, and used them as landmarks, I found that little old hotel where I was staying. The following day, in the afternoon, in the hotel's little bar, I ordered a Coca Cola. While I was drinking it, I noticed in the mirror in front of me over the bar that a group of men, maybe six or eight, were talking and looking at me. Pretty soon, one of the men got up and came over where I was standing and started touching my arms, my shoulders, my waist, and was pointing his finger here and there and talking to the other men. Since he was speaking in English, I didn't know what he was saying. I got worried—what is going on here, I thought. They kept on talking. I finished my Coca Cola just as fast as I could and got out of there.

I forgot all about the incident until that night. Then I was in the dining room having dinner, a man came to my table. He was a big, nice-looking fellow. His first name was Felix. He sat in front of me and started talking to me in Basque, asking me where I was from and that sort of thing. Pretty soon he made a proposal to me. In Basque he said, "Now look if you want to stay here in New York, you can stay right here in this hotel at no cost to you, and you can learn boxing." Right then it occurred to me that these same people, in the afternoon while I was drinking my Coca Cola, were talking about me and about my potential for boxing.

I asked him, "Is that what you people were talking about this afternoon?"

"Yes, that's right," he said, "and we think that you have the potential and so if you want to, you can stay right here in this hotel. It won't cost you anything. We are going to find the people who will train you, teach you, and perhaps you can make a fortune in boxing." At that time, it dawned on me that there were two Basque boxers that were very well-known. One was Juanito Olaguibel, and the other was Paulino Uzkudun. Juanito Olaguibel did not get anywhere. He was punch drunk and we in the Basque Country used to talk about him and crack jokes about him, that every time he heard a ring of a bicycle he started shadow boxing, and when he wasn't doing that he was cutting paper dolls. He was already a ruined man. So I thought if I stayed here maybe something like that would happen to me. Then there was Paulino Uzkudun who actually made a fortune. He fought anybody in America. He became a well-known boxer and a number-one contender for the heavyweight championship of the world. When he came to the U.S. he fought some of the boxers that the white boxers refused to fight, like Dempsey, Sharkey and many others. One of the best known black boxers was Harry Wills. Paulino fought him and knocked him out in the fourth round. Jack Dempsey, to be a champion of the world, didn't have to fight Harry Willis because he was black. Uzkudun fought many others. On his second trip to the U.S., he made a fortune. On the first trip he did not.

As much as I liked to watch boxing, I didn't think that I had what it took to be a boxer—the suspense of waiting to fight someone that I didn't hate. It just wasn't in me. Incidentally, at that time, we worshipped Paulino. He was our idol. But later on, as a result of the Spanish Civil War, Paulino sided in with Franco, and he was one of the crudest fighters against the Loyalist and the Basques, so I despise him to this day. But that is beside the point. At that time, I thought, since I didn't have fighting in my heart, waiting for an opponent that I did not dislike, and fighting it out in the ring for money wasn't for me. My idea of fighting was—and is—when and if I am provoked. It wasn't for me.

So I said, "No, I don't want it. I want to go out west."

This man, Felix, tried to convince me that I should do it, that I should try boxing and perhaps make a fortune, and then he said, "If you don't make it and if you are not good at it, we will put you on the train and you can go west." But I thought, what if I become like Juanito Olaguibel—punch drunk—I wouldn't even be able to herd sheep in the west, so I said no. I was very emphatic and firm. Then we talked about other things, he bought my dinner, and then he left me alone. He told me that in the morning we will put you on the train to go west, and just like Balbuena, he said, "But in the west, young man, you will see nothing but sheep and cows, but if that is what you want I'll see to it that you get on the train tomorrow morning."

He got up, we shook hands, and he left. The following morning, he came to my table while I was having breakfast, early in the morning, and said, "O.K., I will take you to the train." I got my gear, he put me on the right train, and from New York I started to my destination: Boise, Idaho!

It took four days and nights of travel from New York to Boise by train. The trip was uneventful. We changed trains in Chicago. Soon after we were out of the big city, I went to the car designated for smoking. I was the only passenger there, and while I was puffing on my cigarette a porter came in and started to dust the seats and do the necessary cleaning of the coach.

He was a black man. Pretty soon I noticed that he was glancing at me furtively. I could tell by the way he looked at me that he was suspicious of me. Casually he walked towards the door and left the room. That worried me and I went out also to my seat, which was second or third from the front. No doubt that he reported that a suspicious character was traveling on that train, for at the next stop a policeman, accompanied by the conductor, came to my seat and stopped by me. The officer asked me something that I did not understand. Through sign language he made me understand that he wanted me to open the suitcase. I opened it, he searched but found nothing incriminating. I did not have anything to hide. He said something to me and of the long sentence I only understood the word "passport," which is similar to Spanish "pasaporte." I gave it to him, and while he was examining it I could feel the eyes of all the people behind set on me. They were speculating as to what nationality I was because I could understand words like Mexican, Argentinean, Italian, etc., but never Basque.

When the officer got through examining my passport, he returned it to me, smiled, and said something that I did not understand. We shook hands and he left. At that time I did not know the contents of my passport other than it contained my picture and my signature. Much later, after I learned to read English, I realized that, among other things, it stated that, "In case of need, give all lawful aid and protection to Joseph Eiguren, a citizen of the U.S.A." No wonder the officer smiled when he saw that!

There were two or three other men from the Basque Country on the train who were heading to Shoshone, Idaho. Once we arrived in Shoshone and these men got off the train, I was worried, thinking I might miss Boise. I was very alert until I heard the conductor call Boise. Finally I arrived in Boise and stepped off the train, hoping that I would find a familiar face, maybe that of my brother, for he was here in the states for four years. But no, he was not at the depot waiting for me. He was herding sheep in the mountains.

When I arrived in Boise I had between $9-00 and $10.00 left and they were all in nickels and dimes. That is the result of what Father Eguzkiza taught me. Same thing with the taxi. Realizing that there was no one waiting for me I took a taxi. Taxi is a universal word. There were few of them at the depot and again I used what I learned from Father Eguzkiza. I couldn't speak English, but I wrote an address of the place where I was supposed to stay while in Boise.

When I arrived at the home of relatives where I would stay for a few days, the lady of the house, my aunt, wouldn't open the door for me. She did not know me. We had never seen each other. When I knocked on the door, she looked through the peep hole and decided not to let me in because of my appearance. Because of my dark complexion she thought I was one of those Arabians going from door-to-door selling tapestries. I left my suitcase and the trench coat on the porch and staffed towards the city center. When I was about half a block away, I heard someone calling me. It was my aunt. It occurred to her that I was about to arrive in Boise anytime, because we notified her of my impending departure from the Basque Country. She then realized that I was the relative that they (Mr. and Mrs. Joe Navarro) were expecting. I stayed with them for three days in Boise and went to Jordan Valley on the fourth day after my arrival in Boise. A couple who was in Boise visiting friends and relatives gave me a ride. At that time there was no highway from Homedale to Jordan Valley, only a gravel road through Succor Creek Canyon. It took us a whole day to reach Jordan Valley, about twelve hours of driving.

After I got settled in the place where I was to stay temporarily, and I was left alone for a short time, a man entered the house and looked at me, but he didn't say anything. He looked all around him as if he were looking for somebody. Finally, he asked me in Basque, "Where is he?"

I answered him with a question of my own, "Where is who?"

"My brother," he answered.

"I am your brother," I replied. He did not recognize me because of the big change I made physically in the four years since we had seen each other, but I did recognize him. It was a rather emotional encounter.

He stayed in town for three or four days and we had a good visit. I was amazed at his ability to speak English and, in our conversation, I told him how impressed I was. He told me how important it was to learn English if we were going to remain in this country. His advice was as follows: "As a starter, learn to say 'I am sorry, I didn't meant it' and 'thank you,' and you will get by beautifully. The rest will come later."

After this visit, he returned to the sheep camp somewhere in the mountains and we did not see each other very frequently, just occasionally.

6
A New Beginning

I arrived in Jordan Valley during the first part of October, 1934, and was in town until mid-November when I went to the sheep camp for the first time. This was in the fall and there was not much to do except chase the sheep and follow them wherever they were going. This was sort of my on-the-job training program. I was with another man who had several years of experience herding sheep. I didn't know a thing about herding sheep. I was with him only a short time.

In the middle of December, we took the sheep to what we called the "lambing" corrals. I worked there fixing the corrals and cleaning them up for board and room until the lambing started on the 1st of February. Then I started working for wages. I was not very adept at anything related to agriculture or livestock because I did not know anything about it, like cleaning corrals with a pitchfork. Since I grew up on the coast I had more knowledge of fishing and its related industries, not agriculture. The man I was working with had done nothing but clean corrals and pitch hay since he finished high school. He was very adept at that kind of work and he liked to let me know how much better at it he was than I. We were on each side of a horse-drawn manure spreader that we were loading. This was the first time in my life that I had had a pitchfork in my hands. The man on the other side of the spreader threw a pitchfork full of manure all over my head and face. I thought that he did it accidentally. A few minutes later the same thing happened. I began to suspect him. A minute later another pitchfork full of manure was thrown all over me. Then I knew that he was doing it on purpose. I went around the spreader and told him: "Say, you are throwing that manure on me on purpose. You do that again," and pointing my pitchfork at him I told him, "I will stick this on your belly." "Oh, yeah?" he said and laughed. "Try it!" I told him, and went to my side of the spreader. A minute or so later he did it again. Calmly I walked around the spreader holding my fork like one would hold a javelin. When he saw me he got nervous. He knew then that I was going to do what I told him I would do. He ran like a scared jack rabbit. I threw my fork at him, but I missed him because by then he gained some distance. I went to pick my fork up and he said: "You meant what you said, didn't you?"

"Damned right I did. And if you try that again, I'll make sure that I don't miss you the next time."

Perhaps to better understand what herding sheep it all about, I should briefly explain a little bit of the sequence of herding sheep. By the end of February the lambing is pretty much completed; then the next 50 days or so, between the 15th and 20th of March, the lambs are branded. This is called marking to prepare the band to go out, usually by the end of March. Bands usually consist of what we call singles, numbering about 1,000 sheep with their corresponding lambs making a band of approximately 2,000. Then in another band are the twins, which consist of about 800 head of sheep with their twin lambs, making a total of about 2,400 head of animals. They go out on the lower grazing range in the spring. Usually two men go out with the band, the sheep-herder and the camp tender. They move on every day at the speed of the sheep. You don't push them, just let them spread. The camp tender and you move your camp to the front end of the band for the night, gather them around the camp, and the following day they move on again to a fresh pasture. Gradually, the sheep are moved to the higher ground until the summer range is reached, perhaps in the early part of June, and there the sheepherder tries to take advantage of all the good pasture to fatten the lambs as much as possible.

In the first part of July the lambs are shipped. After they are shipped, the sheep (what are known as "dry sheep") are placed together, making a band of 1,800 to 2,000 sheep. After this operation the camp tender is relieved of his duties and the herder is left alone until the last of December, except for some occasional calls by the boss. The sheepherder may see another human once a week, but sometimes he won't see anybody for two weeks or longer.

In September, the sheep are brought down again to what we call the valley. There they graze on irrigated pasture, because the mountain range is completely dry by that time. If it rains early in September, the pastures on the lower range come up good enough to support the dry sheep, so in the last of September, or the early part of October, the sheep go out again to the same place where they grazed early in the spring right after they came out of the corrals until the snow covers the ground or the BLM makes them go in. When I say "in," I mean to the lambing sheds or lambing corrals. The sheepherders clean and fix the corrals for another year's operations and get ready for lambing again.

I did this type of work for six years, and never liked it, but what else could I have done? There were a lot of other things that I would much rather be doing, but I did not have the skills nor the language. I had to sweat it out. To me, this herding sheep was a terrific contrast to the previous years in the Basque Country building fishing boats, to the life in open range taking care of the livestock that I didn't know a thing about. I learned a lot, and I had to learn it the hard way. This was an unusually bad year, I was told, because the sheep developed a disease known as "swell head." We lost a lot of sheep. I skinned literally hundreds of sheep that died as a result of this sickness, and the owner could recover only very little from selling the pelts.

One of the experiences is that when we were in a certain place, high up in the mountains, that I noticed one of our sheep dogs fighting something, but I did not know what it was. The camp tender, called me, "Come on, Kashpar, come on! Look at this!" I went down, and the camp tender explained to me that it was a rattlesnake that the dog was fighting. It was a terrific battle. It was the first time that I had seen a rattlesnake. The snake was finished off by the dog. I had heard that dogs were immune to rattlesnake's bite. Anyway, nothing happened to the dog and the snake was dead.

The camp tender was really a neat fellow, only a year or

two older than I. He knew how to cook, wash his clothes and take care of himself. He spoke perfect Basque even though he was born and raised in the U.S.A. He even knew how to make what we call a "flan" in Basque— some sort of custard. I couldn't believe it how a young fellow like that would know how to cook this complicated thing. I didn't know how to do so many of these things. This particular night, after we saw this fight between the dog and the rattlesnake, he opened his bedroll, shook it, and made sure that there was no rattlesnake in the bedroll. He did this every night. The camp tender's job, I think, was a lot easier than the sheepherder's because all he had to do was move the camp and do the cooking for the both of them and relax, but the sheepherder is walking practically all day. I didn't have the time or desire to unroll my bedroll every night and then fold it again to get into it and sleep. Instead of unrolling it, I tried to get in the bedroll curled and slowly stretch one foot at a time toward the bottom of the bedroll, waiting for something to bite me. If the first leg wasn't bitten, then I stretched the other and I knew there were no rattlesnakes in the bedroll and I would go to sleep.

From this place, we moved towards a higher place named Delamar in the Owyhee Mountains. This was a little bit different from the lower range because it was a sort of juniper forest. When the sheep got in there I got really concerned because they were scattered all over the place and I thought there would be no way that I could gather them like I could in the lower range, with the help of dogs. The camp tender went ahead with his tent, set it up in a certain place, and there I was alone. I was very worried, even scared, thinking that I was going to lose them all. As I was watching the sheep, I saw a man coming towards me on horseback. He spoke to me in Basque. "Kaxio" (Kasheo) —"Hello, there." I don't know how he knew I was a Basque, but probably he assumed that anyone who was herding sheep had to be a Basque. He asked me a few questions:

"Where are you from?"

"I'm from Lekeitio," I told him.

"How long have you been in this country?"

"This is my first year."

He was still mounted on his horse. He was a dark, good-looking guy. He didn't tell me his name. Pretty soon he said, "I'll see you later." He turned around and took off. I was still worried and nervous. In just a few minutes, another man came on horseback. He was approaching me, and maybe from 100 yards or so I recognized him. This man and I went to the same school in the Basque Country. There was quite a bit of difference in age between him and me—he was a lot older, maybe six or seven years. He came and I called him by his name, and he called me by my name. We visited a little bit. He wanted to know when I came and how things were in the Basque Country, as he had been gone from there for a long time. I remembered when he left the Basque Country. He went to Mexico, and from Mexico he came to the U.S. He told me, "Now listen, (he knew right away, and so had the other man, that I was young and inexperienced with the sheep) don't be excited, don't be nervous, let the sheep go wherever they want, and tonight they will bed down right there on top of that hill," and he pointed out where they were going to be. "All you have to do is just go up there. That's all. Don't be chasing them, just relax." Just as he said, as the sun was going down, I could see the sheep going through this slope right to the top of the hill.

I spent the summer of 1935 in this place. I did have the chance to see these two friends that I just mentioned quite often, but other than that I was alone. It was quite bad—a lonely place to be. One of the reasons it was so hard was that the pasture that my boss rented was small, and I had to be after the sheep all the time. These friends of mine had lots of land and sometimes they didn't even see their sheep for three or four days, but from the minute that my sheep got up in the morning from the bedground, until they bedded at night, I had to be after them. Most of the sheepherders usually take a nap or a "siesta" while the sheep are down during the hot part of the day, but I could never do that; I had to be on the move.

One day, when the sheep were down in the creek, I went for a walk, just to see if I could find something different to break the monotony. I came across a cemetery in Wagontown. In this cemetery, I was amazed to find what I did. This cemetery is located three or four miles from Delamar, what used to be a little mining town which was by this time abandoned. There was not a building in this place. However, what I found in the cemetery was truly amazing to me. The cemetery was not kept up at all. It was filled with grass, sagebrush and weeds, and among the tombstones I noticed three Basque surnames. I couldn't believe these people were buried in this remote area of Idaho, and all three of them were born and raised in the Basque Country, came to the U.S., and here they died. One was a twenty-four-year-old man, whose name was Domingo Aldekoa. The other one was Liburia Yturri, a 19-year-old girl, and the third one was Anakabe. I do not remember how old Anakabe was when he died, nor his first name. It depressed me to think they came from the beautiful Basque Country to the U.S. only to die and be buried in that God-forsaken place.

This haunted me for years. What happened to these people? How did they die? Under what circumstances? I found out many years later when I attended a funeral in Jordan Valley. One of the old-timers, with whom I visited, told me the circumstances of their deaths. Domingo Aldekoa, the twenty-four-year-old man, was killed by a cowboy in a place known as Dawn Canyon about eight to ten miles west of Jordan Valley. There was some dispute about the grazing rights, whether the sheep should be grazing there or the cattle. Domingo Aldekoa was a camp tender with a band of sheep, and he had an argument with a cowboy with regards to the rights and according to this man, while he was loading his pack train, the cowboy sneaked up behind him and shot and killed him with a shotgun. Liburia Yturri died in Silver City of pneumonia. Anakabe also was shot and killed, by one of his employees over a salary dispute. Anakabe was a sheepman. He did not die instantly. He was badly wounded, and one of the men, his friend Lazaro Urkiaga, found out, loaded him on a horse and took him to Silver City from Jordan Valley, because there was no doctor in Jordan Valley. Silver City was the closest town that had a doctor at that time. Lazaro took Anakabe there, but it was too late. The doctor could not save him.

7
Encounter with the Trapper

From Delamar we moved the sheep to a place called Cow Creek. Towards the end of August the pasture gets dry, even in the high mountains. Therefore, the sheep have to be moved to the flat irrigated pasture. My boss rented a pasture in Cow Creek, so we moved the sheep over there, about 30 miles from Delamar. Alone I trailed between 2,000 and 2,500 head of sheep in a country that was completely unknown to me. The camp tender gave me the directions, and then went to town. As usual, I followed his directions and got to the designated place in about three days. In the irrigated pasture herding sheep is very easy, for there is a lot of pasture in the meadows after they harvest the hay. I was trailing alone with some stuff to eat, a tepee tent, and a bedroll loaded on the donkey. At night I would catch the donkey, set up camp with the tepee tent, and maybe fry a few eggs, have some coffee and bread, and then hit the sack. In the morning I do the same thing. Eat pretty much the same meal: eggs, bread, and coffee again, and keep going until dark. This place, Cow Creek, was infested with rattlesnakes.

One morning while I was herding sheep in the meadow I saw a man on horseback. I wondered if he was another Basque sheepherder or what we called at that time an American, meaning non-Basque. I thought, what if he is American and comes to meet me? How am I going to get along with him without the language? I wasn't in this country even a year yet, so I couldn't speak English. Sure enough, he was coming towards me, and stopped by me and said something in English, probably "Hello, there." I replied with a "Good morning" in Spanish, thinking that Spanish is closer to English than it is the Basque. After our first encounter, he came to see me quite often. Most of the time at mealtime, lunchtime, and suppertime. He hardly had anything to eat. He was a trapper and came to that area to set up some traps for coyotes and bobcats. In spite of our language barrier, we got along fairly good. He was a man in his middle sixties. I was twenty years old at the time.

While I was herding sheep in this place, I had the opportunity to go to town to get a haircut. This was the first time in six months that I had a chance to do so. I went on horseback to Jordan Valley, which is a distance of 15 to 20 miles. I got a haircut and returned the following day. During the time I stayed in Jordan Valley I got $5.00 or $10.00 from the man I was working for. The sheepherders were paid once a year, and whenever we needed anything while we were in the mountains (such as tobacco, clothing, shoes, etc.), the boss would buy it for us and he would keep track of what he bought and at the end of the year we got paid what we had earned, minus what we had taken in advance. When I returned to the sheep camp, I remember distinctly that I had $3.47 left. When my friend the trapper came to see me, somehow he found out that I had this money left and he wanted that money badly to buy some things he didn't have, such as flour, sugar, coffee, etc. He was living on jack-rabbits and what he called flapjacks. He told me that he would like to go to town if he had some money to buy these items. Just as soon as he found out that I had a little money, he decided that he wanted it and he instigated a card game hoping that he would get it from me. The game we played was solitaire. I was a little familiar with that game. I never did like to play cards, but my mother learned to play solitaire in the U.S. and I used to see her playing it so I knew a little bit about it. Fred, my friend, and I started playing. At that time, Fred had only one coyote's pelt and one bobcat's pelt. He gave a value of $2.00 to the bobcat's pelt and for each face card I was to pay him five cents. I agreed. We proceeded our game on these terms. I beat him and he felt sad about it. I got the pelt of the bobcat. Then we talked, and somehow we came to an agreement that he was going to give a value of $3.00 to the coyote's pelt, and I was to pay five cents for each face card. We proceeded playing, and I beat him again. He was so sad. He was talking sort of to himself. I didn't know what he was saying, but from the expression on his face, I knew that he was feeling very sad. I kept him that way out of orneriness, I guess. Maybe I was looking for some sort of excitement in this monotonous life of herding sheep. When he was just about ready to leave, I gave him back his pelts, the cat's and the coyote's, and $3.45. I kept two cents because I knew that he couldn't buy anything with two cents. I could see by the expression on his face how happy he was. He kept on talking, but I didn't know what he was saying. That evening while I was herding sheep, I saw him going towards town with his old wagon and his old horse. We waved at each other, and soon he was gone from sight. Then as usual, after dark I got the sheep bedded and went to bed.

I was awakened by a mixture of rifle shots and somebody yelling, screaming, and singing about one or two o'clock in the morning. I got up out of the bedroll, put on my jeans and shoes, and went to where the sound was coming from. It was my friend, Fred. There he was, drunk, in the old house where he was staying that was lit with a kerosene lamp. As I approached him, he recognized me and started talking. He had a bottle of whiskey in one hand and a rifle in the other. He extended the bottle to me. I grabbed it and took a big snort and returned the bottle to him. Between the two of us we killed the bottle in no time. Then he lay down and went to sleep. I put him on the cot, removed his shoes and took the rifle away from him. I went back to my bedroll and to sleep.

With the money that he got from selling the cat and the coyote's pelt in Jordan Valley, plus the $3.45 I gave him, he didn't buy any groceries as he said he would. He got drunk and bought a bottle of whiskey to bring with him to the camp. He didn't buy any sugar, flour, coffee, potatoes, macaroni or tomatoes—nothing, absolutely nothing—but a bottle of whiskey. The following day when we got together he was apologetic for what had taken place the previous day. I did feel sorry for the man. He didn't have any more pelts to sell.

Soon after that, I had to move with the sheep to another place which was known as Danner. Because the pasture where I was at in Cow Creek was just about gone, I had to move to another place, an alfalfa pasture. It was about 15 or 20 miles from Cow Creek to Danner. I told my friend that I was leaving soon. He felt that he wanted to reciprocate by having me as a guest for dinner for all the dinners and lunches he had with me. So one evening I went to his place for dinner! He was cooking outside of the old, abandoned shack. He had these so-called flapjacks and a couple of skinny jackrabbits, almost raw. I wasn't sure whether I could eat that stuff. Due to courtesy, I thought I was going to try to eat with him. I had a bite or two. I just couldn't eat the bloody jackrabbits. Pretty soon I excused myself, went by the creek, and threw up. When the big affair was over, I went back to my tent for the night, and the following day I left for Danner with my band of sheep.

There, the camp tender came again, picked up the camp or the tent, left a few groceries, a frying pan, some coffee, a donkey, and a bedroll, then went on to town. I spent a couple of days and nights from Cow Creek to Danner by myself with the tepee tent, a bedroll, a few eggs, some bread, and coffee.

When I got to Danner I met the camp tender there. He showed me where the tent was and told me how to herd sheep in alfalfa. In alfalfa, believe it or not, one must scientifically herd sheep. Let me explain. Sheep are dumb, stupid animals. If they ate turned loose in the alfalfa they would all die, for they don't know when they have had enough to eat! They would eat and eat until they got bloated and then die. The way to herd them is let them go to the alfalfa pasture and stop them in a certain area and slowly rake them out of the pasture in less than seven minutes. That is, you allow them in and out of the pasture in seven minutes. After seven minutes, there is a danger that every damn one of them will die. That is how stupid they are. That's what I was doing on this afternoon after I got to Danner. I'd let the sheep eat and I would get in front of them with my dog. After four minutes or so I would start driving them out. While you are driving them out slowly, if any one of the lambs (not the sheep because you don't eat sheep) should happen to be bloated, you butcher them before they fall down. If you do that, you can use the lamb for your own consumption. If they should fall down and die, then you are not supposed to eat them.

While I was watching, there was one beautiful lamb that I thought was not going to make it. I was sure that it was going to fall down. It was wobbling, so when I realized that it was going to fall, I got to it and butchered it. While I was skinning it, I was still watching the sheep. I had a watch in one hand and a knife in the other. And while simultaneously watching the sheep and butchering a lamb, I accidentally jabbed my left leg with the knife rather deeply and cut an artery. I knew I was in trouble. I raised up my pant leg and saw that I was bleeding profusely. I didn't have any idea how to stop the bleeding. I pulled a dirty handkerchief out of my pocket and wrapped it around the wound. At the same time I tried to get the sheep out of the alfalfa field. My boss happened to be there and took charge of the sheep. He didn't know how to stop the bleeding either. I looked around and saw a crew of men working on stacking hay. I started hopping toward the haystack on my one leg which was the right leg. I started going just as fast as I could. I don't know how far I went, perhaps a quarter of a mile, to where the crew on the stack was working, before I blacked out and fell down. That was the end of Kashpar, I thought. Luckily, from the haystack a man spotted me and probably realized that something was wrong. He came over to where I was with his car. He was a small, wiry man. A really good man. His name was Dale Sinclair. He had me in his arms and was putting me in his car when I came to. I looked at my leg and saw some contraption below my knee. Later on I found out that was what they called a tourniquet. At the time I did not know.

He took me to his house and when we arrived there he stepped out of the car and went into the house. Soon he and his wife, Jessie, came out together. He evidently had explained to her what had happened. She went back to the house and got some hot water and some clean pieces of rags, washed my leg which was full of blood, talking incessantly. I never understood what she was saying. After she fixed my leg up, Dale Sinclair got hold of my hand and placed it on the tourniquet. I'm sure that he was trying to explain to me that if it started bleeding to tighten it up, and as long as it was not bleeding to loosen it up in order for the blood to circulate. Otherwise it could easily have turned into gangrene. I think I understood him and I tried to do what he said. Then he had to go back to the haystack to take care of the haying crew, as he was the owner of the ranch.

He asked his brother, Sterling Sinclair, to take me to town. Sterling was unable to work as he was asthmatic and had a lot of trouble being around animals and alfalfa. Dale's brother Sterling took me to Jordan Valley to see a doctor. The doctor was out of town, so Sterling took me to the C.C.C. camp. As I was walking away from the car to the infirmary, I started bleeding again. Three or four medics grabbed me and put me on a cot and proceeded to stop my bleeding by applying pressure to my groin. They couldn't stop it by this method, so finally they decided to tighten the tourniquet. Through an interpreter they all wanted to know how I felt. Did I have pain? No, I didn't feel any pain. Finally, after so many questions, I told them that I was hungry. They brought me a bunch of crackers and hot chocolate. Just then the young C.C.C. doctor came in. He looked at me and talked to me for a while. All I needed to stop that bleeding was just one stich which the doctor proceeded to do. He bandaged my leg and I was ready to leave.

I was taken to my relatives' home where I stayed until I recovered. It took me almost a month to recover from the incident. One day while I was recovering I heard someone singing coming towards our house. I recognized the man. It was my friend the trapper, Fred Gilbert. He found out that I was hurt so he decided to come and visit me. I don't know what we talked about, but when he left he pulled out a five-dollar bill and left it on the nightstand for me. I tried to tell him that I didn't want it, but he just laughed at me. He knew I couldn't do anything about it because I could hardly move. He stood up, we shook hands, and he left. This was the last time I saw my friend, Fred. He left the $5.00 in payment of the two pelts that I had given him plus the $3.45.

8
A Lonely Life

The life of a sheepherder is nothing spectacular. I think a lot of people think it is really interesting, and perhaps even romantic. I didn't find it that way. To me it was a monotonous, lonely life; I never did like it. I always thought I wanted to do something else, but what? Where would I go? No language. No money. The whole country was in a deep depression, and a lot of people were without a job. A guy like me without the language, what else could I have done? I often thought that I wanted to go to the mining camps, but there were a lot of miners out of a job. Men with experience and able to speak the language were out of a job, so how could I compete with them? I even thought that I would like to work in a lumber camp, as I was used to that kind of work, but there was no way that I could quit herding sheep and go looking for another job knowing that I would never find one. There was absolutely nothing to do but chase those stupid, idiotic, filthy sheep day and night, seven days a week for 365 days a year. I remember the man who I was working for told me several times, in Basque, "There is no place better than Jordan Valley in America for a person to work and save money." He said that over and over again.

One time I told him, "Well, in the United States of America there is something like 200,000,000 people, so how come there are only 150 people or less in Jordan Valley if it is such a damn good place to make money? Where did the rest of them go? Why didn't they come here?" He had a silly grin and didn't know what to say.

Soon after I came to this country and went herding sheep, if I had had enough money and if there was a train going through the Antelope Mountains where I was herding sheep, I would have climbed on it and left the sheep and gone back to Lekeitio where I came from. But it wasn't that easy. I had to make the best of it. I thought maybe as time went by something would develop that might change my lifestyle.

I found out that there was a Spanish newspaper published in New York named *La Prensa.* Since I was not able to read English, I thought I would subscribe to that, and so I told the man for whom I was working that I would like to have a subscription to that newspaper. He arranged it, and I started getting it. The newspaper came two or three weeks late all the time, but it was better than nothing. Through it I learned about the 1936 Spanish Civil War in Spain and in the Basque Country. I also learned through this newspaper that there was a delegation from the Basque Country in Vera Cruz, Mexico, and that their mission was to recruit volunteers to fight Franco. According to the accounts I read, three or four hundred Mexicans had volunteered to go and fight with the Loyalists. I wrote a letter telling of my desire to join them, and received an answer from the Basque delegation saying that I could be of more help by contributing financially to their cause. They didn't understand. They figured that this guy Kashpar had been in the United States for 24 months, he was making $40 a month, and $40 a month for 24 months comes out to be $960. These people figured that I had $960, and that I should send it to them to help them financially, not realizing the money I had borrowed to come to this country and other expenses that I had incurred, such as buying my bedroll, shoes and clothing. So I gave up the idea of going to fight against Franco. I thought that if they would accept me as a volunteer to go and fight Franco that they would help me pay my debts and transportation to Vera Cruz, Mexico, and then I would go with them to Spain and fight for the Basque cause. That was not possible. They did not have the money either.

Through this newspaper, I learned that Gernika the holy city of the Basques, was destroyed by the German Condor Legion. By the time I got *La Prensa,* it was old news, but for me it was new. I was really sad when I started thinking about my mother, my relatives, and all my friends who were Basque nationalists. I wanted to be with them, fighting these Fascist, murderous Germans and Italians, but it was not possible. I remember distinctly where I was when I read this in the paper. I was in the Antelope Mountains herding sheep, and for the first time in my life I heard mourning doves, and even today when I hear them it depresses me. Whenever I hear them, I think of the destruction of Gernika and its people scurrying all over, running away from the town, and the German planes chasing them, strafing and machine gunning them down.

After Franco's victory in 1939, I realized that there was no chance for me to go back to the Basque Country. I would never go and live under Franco and the Fascist dictatorship, and I realized that I would probably be here in the United States forever. I decided that in order to remain here I would have to learn to speak English. Through some advertisements in *La Prensa* I found that there was a method named Método Cortina, (that is, Cortina's Method), on "How to Learn to Speak English in Twenty Lessons," and also a Spanish/English and English/Spanish dictionary. I asked the man for whom I was working to order these books for me, pay for it, and then have it charged to me. That is how I started to learn English, but it was difficult. I was able to make out some grammatical aspects, but I did not have anyone to practice with. I remember one time that I was in a place in the summer range, a place known as Owl Creek in the Owyhee Mountains, and was reading the newspaper, *La Prensa,* and came across a word that was not familiar to me in Spanish. The word was "anfitrión." I looked in the dictionary and couldn't find it in the Spanish part. I often made up a lot of words just by guessing, so since "anfitrión" was not in the Spanish part, I thought there might be the same word in English by changing the stress from the last syllable in Spanish to the second syllable in English. But I couldn't find it in the English part either. I got so mad with the dictionary that I put it on the block that I used to chop wood and chopped it to pieces with the ax. There was paper flying all over the place. I thought I was going to have a heart attack, I worked so hard destroying it.

When I started to learn English on my own, I took a very

strong interest. The problem was that I did not have anybody to practice with. I subscribed to a very popular magazine at that time: *Liberty* and I tried to read it. The words that I couldn't understand I underlined them and at night, by candlelight I looked them up in the dictionary. This way I came to certain conclusions, namely (for example): the English words like "probable" is the same in Spanish "probable" with the difference that in Spanish the second syllable is stressed and in English the first syllable is stressed. Then, to convert these words into adverbs the word probable is converted to "probably" and in Spanish it is changed to "probablemente." So I came to the conclusion that those words that ended in "ly" in English, in Spanish are ending "-mente." Also I realized that words that end in "-ty" like "possibility" in Spanish are ended in "-dad" "posibilidad." There are many examples that could be cited. When I overcame that big obstacle I felt like dancing just like King David danced in the streets of Jerusalem after he defeated Goliath. It was a big victory for me!

Even though it was customary to settle accounts once a year, we settled ours after the two years I herded sheep. I don't remember the itemized expenses, but from the time I started working, which was February 1935, to September 1937, I paid the money that I had borrowed from my Uncle Pasko to come to the United States. I paid him the $400 I owed him—and other expenses that I had incurred in buying my bedroll, clothes, tobacco, and the money that I had sent to my mother, for she was alone and we had to help her.

I was left with $29, and of this $29 I gave $25 to my aunt, a lady with whom I stayed whenever I came to Jordan Valley. After paying everything, at the end of two years of herding sheep I was left with $4. I was happy that I did not owe anything to anybody and able to help my mother all I could. FOUR DOLLARS! At the end of two years of herding sheep! And my boss tells me that there was no place like Jordan Valley to make money!

Kashpar and his brother Domingo (Txomin) in the Americas before getting married.

In the next two years herding sheep at the rate of $60.00 per month I earned $1,440.00.

Sometime in August of 1939 I found out that there were 900 head of sheep for sale at $2.00 per head and they could be purchased by paying $1.00 per head as a down payment. I had enough money saved to make the down payment and some left to buy other necessities like a donkey, a tent, some cooking utensils, etc. I told one of my friends, an older man, about what I was thinking and he not only encouraged me, but offered to help me financially if I needed help.

"I like young men who think on these lines" he said. "Go at it." I always regarded this man highly and considered him my friend, not because of his spontaneous offer to help me, but from much before. He was the man that gave me my first job in America. It was not much of a job, just cleaning his business premises of litter and burying litter on his property, and this man paid me more for that day and a half than I was earning in nine days in the Basque Country working from daylight to dark. This man was Joe Berrojalbiz, better known perhaps by the nickname of "Estudio."

The problem was that I couldn't do it alone. I needed a partner who spoke English to run the business, like to buy pasture if needed, hay for the winter, bring groceries to me, etc. So I approached a man a little older than me and asked him if he would be interested in going in partners with me in the sheep business. This man didn't have a thing. He was out of a job, did not have money to pay for his board and room, absolutely nothing but a pair of shoes with holes the size of silver dollars in its soles, which was the result of his pounding the streets of Boise looking for a job that did not exist. I asked him if he would like to be a partner in my "stock raising" enterprise.

He said, "No, we better not go in sheep business."

"Why not?" I asked him.

"Because we will go broke," he replied!

"What do you mean by 'we'll go broke?' What do you have to invest in the partnership? You have nothing to invest, therefore nothing to lose. If we do go broke it will be me, not you."

That ended our conversation and any ideas of going into

the sheep business.

My cousin, whose father I was working for, always made fun of everything about me—my lack of knowledge of herding sheep, other agricultural aspects, and particularly the size of my feet. For example, when I first arrived in Jordan Valley, he took me to buy a pair of shoes. When the salesman asked what size I needed I told him "37's" which was the way European sizes ran. Both men laughed and laughed while I stood there in embarrassment wondering what was so funny. My cousin told the clerk, "This guy doesn't need shoes, he needs boats." I asked him what was so funny, and he translated what he had said to the clerk. From then on I was always conscious of the size of my feet and always bought shoes size 9-1/2, even though I needed 10-1/2 or 11. I really suffered. I had heard from other sheepherders that the best way to stretch your shoes was to fill them with beans and add water and let them set overnight. When the beans swelled, the shoes would stretch. I tried it, and it worked as far as the width was concerned but the shoes were still too short, so I poked holes in front of my big toes so that they could stick out which really looked comical, but at least they were comfortable. And this guy tells everybody that he taught me how to speak English. I don't remember ever trying to speak English in his presence, for fear of being ridiculed.

9
Small Incidents at the Sheep Camp

When herding sheep in the mountains, nothing spectacular ever happened, just small insignificant things from time to time. When a person looks back, some things seem to be comical.

One time I ran out of tobacco. I had been smoking cigarettes since I was 13. I ran out of tobacco, and thought that was something catastrophic. What was I going to do? I was alone in the mountains, there was no one around, and I couldn't borrow a can of Prince Albert or Velvet or any other kind of tobacco. It just occurred to me that some of the older sheepherders, whenever we were together in the wintertime talking about various things, mentioned a certain plant that was actually a sunflower, and the old sheepherders called it "tobacco leaves." I gathered leaves of sunflowers and burned them until they were crisp, pounded them into powder and rolled them up in cigarette paper and smoked. It was awful! It was so strong that it was impossible to inhale, but I kept at it for a week or longer. Then I remembered somebody saying that some other sheepherder in the same predicament as I was substituted coffee for tobacco. He ground the coffee, rolled it in a cigarette paper and smoked it. I started doing that and found that it was a lot better than the sunflower leaves that I was using. It was not as good as real tobacco, but it was much better than sunflowers! I smoked the coffee until the camp tender came and took my order to bring tobacco the next time he came, which would be in another week. He was not going to come just to bring me tobacco all the way to the mountains.

After waiting two weeks without smoking, what I should have done was quit. If at that time there was as much information as there is now on how harmful tobacco is, I would have quit easily, but we thought tobacco was a healthy thing, especially to smoke after meals and after a cup of coffee. Besides, we thought it was a smart thing to do, so I continued smoking. When the camp tender did come with the tobacco, I thought I had to catch up for all the days that I had been without it.

Another incident that might be interesting occurred one day when I received a letter from my girlfriend from the Basque Country. For a long time I had not received any letters from her because of the Spanish Civil War. I was glad to hear all about her and her family. In this letter, among other things, she told me that their family was in a bad predicament, and they wanted to escape to France because her father was on the black list of Franco, and if they caught him he would be executed. I well remember her father. He was a real radical element. I think he was the only man that never attended the church in that town where I grew up. I don't know what political affiliation he belonged to, but I do know that it was a very radical element, and because of that Franco's side was going to execute him as they had so many others. I saw this man every day in Lekeitio. He knew that his daughter, Carmen, and I were going together, but he never spoke to me. He had the meanest look. In this letter, Carmen asked me if I would loan them some money to help their dad get out of Spain. She asked me for $300. That was a lot of money at that time, and that was exactly the amount that I had saved by then. From the $300 that she asked me for, I sent her $250 and kept $50, like the saying here, "for a rainy day." I did hear from her later saying that they managed to cross the Pyrenees on foot, the whole family, and entered France as refugees. As I have said before, this man never spoke to me, but when this happened, he wrote me a letter, a really neat letter. I don't remember the contents exactly but he acknowledged the receipt of the money and how much he appreciated it. I was glad that I was able to help them.

At about the same time, I also received a letter from a friend of mine, one of the guys with whom I had gone to school, Alberto Madariaga. When I received the letter I didn't know who was writing it because I could hardly read it, it was so badly writ-ten. Finally, I figured out the contents. The reason it was so badly written was that in the Civil War he had lost his right arm at the shoulder as a result of a German shell, a direct hit that tore his right arm off at the shoulder. They saved his life. He had to learn to write with his left hand. I felt so sorry for him that I almost cried. He had written this letter from France. He was also a refu-gee of the Spanish Civil War. I answered his letter and sent him ten dollars, and from time to time I would send him five or ten dollars in my letters to him as long as we maintained correspon-dence. Alberto never asked me for any money. I knew instinc-tively that he needed or could use some. Alberto was an extraor-dinary man. His appearance was arresting. He was about 6 foot, 200 pounds with a prominent chin jutted out, pushing his lower teeth over his upper teeth giving him the erroneous impression of being a mean man. He was the kindest man I had ever known.

The reason I wanted to go back to the Basque Country during the Civil War was because all my friends were there, and all but one were fighting against Franco, and I wanted to join them. But it didn't work out.

One summer while I was herding sheep alone, I happened to be in a very deep canyon, and in the late afternoon when the sheep started moving up I started going up toward the top of the mountain to bed them down. As the sheep moved out, there was one old, sick sheep that couldn't keep up with the others. I de-cided to pick up the old ewe which weighed 125 pounds or more. I put her on my back and chased the band from four o'clock in the afternoon until almost dark with that old ewe on my back, on and off. When we got to the place where I was going to bed the sheep, I put the sheep down, caught the donkey, unrolled the bedroll, and lay down on it. I was exhausted and hungry, but too tired to fix anything to eat. While I was resting, thinking that I might eat something later, I almost fell asleep. I noticed that there was just one star in the sky. I remembered that somebody told me, probably that trapper I mentioned or some other old cowboy, that if you see a lonely star in the evening and if you make a wish, that wish will come true. I happened to think of that while I was lying there with my hands clasped at the back of my head looking up at the sky and the star, and I decided to make a wish. I was almost embarrassed even to make a wish like that, because I was sure that it was not possible for such a wish to ever come true. I looked around furtively in the God-forsaken place to see if there was someone watching me. There was not a soul there and I knew it, so I went ahead and made my wish. The wish was that a girl that I met in Jordan Valley just a few days after I arrived in this country would be my wife someday. I know how ridiculous that sounds. She was so pretty and so popular and she had so many pretenders, well-to-do people wanting to date her. How could poor old "Succor Creek Joe" compete with them?

The first time I saw this girl was one evening when I was going to town from the place where I was living in Jordan Valley and noticed that there were two girls, but I couldn't see their faces for it was dark. One of the girls I had already met called me by my name. I went towards them, and we started talking. Both of these girls spoke perfect Basque, just like natives. I asked the girl I had met before to tell me who this other girl was, and she told me her name, but I couldn't see her face. I struck a match so I could see her and when I did I thought she was the prettiest thing that I had ever seen in my life. From that moment on, she was always on my mind. I also thought it was preposterous to think that my wish would ever come true. Her name was Aurora.

10
A Sheepherder's Fear and Other Changes

I suppose that all jobs have certain aspects, good and bad. The same is true with herding sheep. There are certain seasons that ate better than others, but even the better ones are not good as a sheepherder for me.

As far as I am concerned, there was no part of herding sheep that was good to me. Even though all the seasons were bad, the best season was winter. That is the time that sheepherders are getting ready for lambing and are among other people. At that time there are certain entertainments or distractions from time to time during lambing. Sometimes we get to go to a dance, to town or some grange hall or the schoolhouse of a ranching community. Springtime was the worst as I have described earlier. The summer is not too bad if one happened to be in a place where there was plenty of good pasture, which I never was! The autumn was not too bad, except that the sheepherder is alone for long periods, sometimes for a week, ten days, or even longer without seeing another human being.

One of the things that sheepherders worry about most in the fall is fog. If it rains, for a couple of days in the first part of September and then the weather turns warm, the grass in the open range turns green and makes very good pasture for the sheep. Then the sheepherders go out with the sheep, grazing on range until the last day of December, if the snow doesn't cover the grass sooner.

A typical day of the sheepherder in the fall under the

conditions described is like this: Sheep move out at daylight and the sheepherder sends the band in the direction he wants them to graze. Then he fixes and eats his breakfast; chops some wood, and puts it in the tent to keep it dry. He goes to the creek and fills his water bags with water. (Often he has to break the ice in the creek with an ax and fill the bags with a cup.)

This is the only type of tent I used in my six years of herding sheep. Notice the rifle to the sheepherders left, the towel and wash basin, and the indispensable Dutch oven.

I didn't know how to wash clothes, so in hot weather I never wore anything but jeans and shoes. I did not wear socks, shorts, or shirts for two reasons: I did not know how to wash them and didn't like to wash them. My system of washing, when the weather permitted, was to soap the items good and place them in the creek anchored with rocks. Then, when I returned after a long day of walking with the sheep, I picked up my "laundry" and hung it on top of sage brush to dry. After these chores were done he picks up his lunch and a rifle and goes chasing the sheep, usually by bypassing the band without disturbing it. He goes way ahead of the band and waits there until the sheep approach him. Around 2:00 p.m. or so the herder turns the band in the direction of the bedground and goes back to the tent which is located in the bedground. He cooks supper in the candlelight while listening to the radio (if he has one). He may read old newspapers, *La Prensa,* eat supper, read some old, cheap, dime novels like *Shadow,* which I often did, most of the time not knowing what I was reading. I would have to look in the English-Spanish dictionary for words that I did not understand while reading the novels. Then he would go to bed, listening to the sheep blatting and the coyotes howling until he went to sleep.

This autumn day was no different from any other that I have described, except that when I got up in the morning and stepped out of the tent, I scanned the horizon all around me, and from all indications I knew that we were going to have a very nasty, foggy day. I thought that perhaps I should take some precautions to avoid getting lost in the fog. My tent was only about a hundred yards from a trail or a rough dirt mountain road. I sent the sheep on, did my chores and went to the trail. Since the direction I gave to the band was parallel with the trail, I followed the trail. I pulled out the biggest sagebrush from the ground and put it upside down, roots up on another brush. I followed the trail for at least three miles and every 100 or 150 yards of the first half-mile I pulled up a sagebrush and placed it upside down. I was trying to create a "trail" of sagebrush to follow on my return to my tent so I wouldn't get lost.

It was only a matter of two or three hours before the whole area was covered with very thick fog. About 2:00 p.m. I decided that it was time to turn the sheep towards the bedground. I stepped out of the trail but because of the density of the fog I only went about a hundred yards before visibility was nil and I was afraid that I was going to get lost if I went any further.

Often, in order to turn the sheep in the direction you want, all you need to do is fire a few shots in the air with your rifle and induce your dogs to bark. I did exactly that and carefully returned to the trail and started walking toward my tent. I found the first upside down brush, followed the trail and about dusk reached my tent. Observing outside of the tent, I could tell from the sheep's blatting and their bells ringing that the band was split but coming in the right direction toward the bedground. I got in the tent, built a fire on the stove and turned the radio on.

On this occasion I did have a radio, a battery-operated

radio that belonged to the camp tender, my cousin. I was not able to find the usual programs on the radio. Every station that I turned on was saying something about Pearl Harbor . . . American Navy . . . bombing . . . and so on. I knew from what I could gather that something big had happened, but I did not know what for sure. This was December 7, 1941, the day Pearl Harbor was bombed by the Japanese, but I did not know it for sure until several days later, perhaps a week or ten days later when my boss came and told me about it. Right then and there I made up my mind that I was going to quit herding sheep and join the U.S. military services, preferably the Navy, but I did not tell my boss at the time. I waited until we went into the lambing corrals on the last day of December. The day after I arrived at the ranch, which was New Year's Day of 1942, I told my boss that I was quitting and that I was going to join the Navy, and I asked him to take me to town. He thought I was crazy. He asked me, "Are you out of your mind?" "No, I am not," I replied. "I am serious."

He proceeded to tell me that he had plans for me and that I shouldn't do such a stupid thing like enlist in the Navy. He told me that he was getting older and that he thought that he was going to turn his business over to his son, who was my cousin, and me in a year or two. I told him I wanted no part of it and that I wanted to join the Navy now. He told me that he wasn't going to take me to town.

"In that case," I told him, "I will find someone who will take me."

When he realized that I meant business, he said that he would take me to town, and so he did. From Jordan Valley I went to Boise, and with the help of an interpreter (who was my cousin Emilia, my boss's daughter), I went to a Navy recruitment office in Boise to enlist. I was rejected because I couldn't speak English well enough. There I was, no job nor military service, but I felt pretty optimistic that before too long I would be called to serve in our armed services in some capacity and I was right. Within six weeks a letter arrived from Franklin Delano Roosevelt stating: "My dear Fellow American: Greetings . . . etc., etc., etc. I was very happy, and eager, to be a member of our armed services. I was drafted!

11
Farewell Party

While in Boise waiting for the day that I was supposed to report to Vale for my induction, I received an invitation to go to Jordan Valley on the 12th or 13th of March to attend a farewell party that the people of Jordan Valley were giving the boys that were to leave for the Army. There were seven of us men scheduled to leave soon. When I had an opportunity to go to Jordan Valley, I did.

The farewell party was celebrated at one of the dance halls. It was a very interesting affair. Practically the whole town attended to say goodbye to the seven draftees who were to report in Vale the following day after the party. The party started out rather early in the evening. There was a lot to drink and eat and a lot of dancing. I did not know very many people, in spite of the fact that I was in that area of Jordan Valley for six years, because in all those six years I didn't spend much time in town. Since I didn't know very many people, I stayed back in the corner watching what was going on, people dancing and drinking. After I had a few snorts, I danced several times with different girls, but for the most part I stayed pretty much to myself. As the party was in progress and coming to the early-morning hours, one man, a big fellow, called for attention. "Okay, boys, it's time to go," he said. "It is five in the morning and it will take us two hours or longer to get to Vale, so we must be on our way."

Everything stopped! People began to kiss their relatives goodbye, friends started kissing their loved ones who were about to leave. While watching all these activities I noticed a girl coming toward me. She stopped by me and told me in Basque, "I came to tell you goodbye."

I said thank you. We were looking at each other, and our eyes locked like magnets. She was very pretty. She was short, maybe 5'2". She extended her hand, and I took it. We shook hands. Pretty soon she moved closer and placed her hand on the back of my neck and kissed me. "Agur," she said, which means goodbye in Basque. I was so surprised! Then she asked me, 'Are you going to write to me?"

I answered, "If I knew that you would answer my letters, I would."

She replied, "I will answer every letter that you write me, I promise."

"Then I will write to you," I replied.

By now the hall was practically empty. She and I walked together to where automobiles and some friends were waiting to take us to Vale. We said goodbye again, shook hands, and she said, "Take care of yourself, Kashpar, and good luck to you. Return home just as soon as you can." I thanked her and got in the car and we were off.

All the time on our trip I was thinking of her. We traveled in a sort of caravan. There were seven of us boys and some friends and relatives. There must have been four or five cars at least.

In Vale, we were taken to some offices for proper identification and a physical examination. From there we were taken to the train depot where we met a lot of other people who were drafted from Malheur County—people from Vale, Ontario, Nyssa, Juntura and many other towns that comprise Malheur County, all waiting for the train.

While we were waiting, an older man came to me and said to me in Basque, "Kaxio Gaste" "Hello there, young man." I don't know how he knew I was Basque; I guess we just recognized each other by the shape of our noses or some other physical characteristic. He introduced himself as Vincent Mendiola. We talked a little bit and then he said, "I will be right back, I have to get something. I'll see you a little later." And he left. Sure enough, about fifteen minutes later he came back and brought me a fifth of whiskey as a going-away present. I'd never seen the man before, and I never saw him again. He wished me good luck, we shook hands, and he left.

Kashpar while receiving nine weeks of training at the Santa Barbara Polo Grounds.

From Vale we were taken to Salt Lake City and then to Fort Douglas where we were inducted on March 16, 1942. In the process of induction, there were many things that we had to go through. One of them was an I.Q. test. They gave me an I.Q. test, but I could barely read or write English. Still, it was surprising how much of it I could understand. I understood some of the words because of the similarity of some of the English and Spanish words. I knew that my I.Q. couldn't be very high. I often wonder or would have liked to have known the results of that I.Q. test. I was assigned to the infantry and served for four years.

From Salt Lake City, we were sent to Santa Barbara, California, for our basic training, where we received nine weeks of training at the Santa Barbara Polo Grounds. The conditions there were incredibly bad. Living quarters for privates and non-commissioned officers consisted of 16 x 16 foot pyramid tents. The officers were quartered at the stables or barns where horses were kept previously. We didn't have water in our tents, only a cold water faucet maybe a block away. We shaved and washed with cold water using our helmets for containers. About twice a week we had to take a shower in cold water whether we liked it or not, since that was all that was available. The non-commissioned officers herded us, a company at a time, to the stables to take showers. The food was bad. We ate out of our mess kits. Food was nothing like what we would have in the regular Army camp. The training was very intense. Of course, I was in good shape when I went in with all of those years of climbing those mountains, herding sheep, pitching hay in the winter, and that kind of exercise. So the training didn't bother me much. But there were other men who had lived in town who found it very hard to adjust. At the completion of the basic training, we were sent to Watsonville, also in California. Our duties from that time on were to patrol the California coast all the way from Santa Barbara to San Francisco on Highway # 1, the coastal highway and surrounding outposts. From the moment we finished our basic training, our regiment was on full field duty, living as if we were in combat and eating field rations, not in a regular Army base.

12
Life in the Army

After I arrived in Santa Barbara and got settled in these tents, I had a little spare time so I wrote my first letter in English to that girl I promised I would write to when I left Jordan Valley. I did receive an answer to my letter from the girl. From then on, every letter that I wrote, she answered. After we left Santa Barbara, we were sent to our first assignment in Watsonville. The first letter that I received in Watsonville from the girl included a one dollar bill that she told me she was sending so I could go to a show. I was so impressed! I wanted to have something to remember her by, so I saved the dollar bill and never did use it for a show or for anything else. Even today I have it with me.

After three months of patrolling the California coast up and down, manning a few outposts in the beach sand dunes like Half Moon Bay, Moro Bay, Pismo Beach and several other places, I had a chance for the first time, to go to Jordan Valley on furlough. I traveled by train to San Francisco, crossed the Bay on the ferry, boarded the train in Oakland, and left for Salt Lake City. At the time we departed from Oakland, it was lunchtime. Soon after we left Oakland, a fellow went from car to car announcing that this was the last call for dinner (that was the midday meal). I was pretty hungry but I always heard that eating on a train was very expensive, and I didn't have too much money. I wasn't sure if I even had enough money to pay for the lunch. I didn't know what to do. I waited too long. Finally I decided to go, but by the time I got to the dining coach it was too late, and the regular dining time was over. However, there was a special group in the dining room so I opened the door and went in. I was amazed at what I saw. When I got into the dining coach, the place was full of men, all black. There must have been forty or more of them. I was walking through the aisle looking for a place to sit down, but they were all taken. I could feel some furtive looks from the black men, like they were saying, "What is this guy doing here?" I kept on moving and just about in the middle of the dining coach I spotted one man on my right side alone. In front of him was an empty seat. In my best English I asked him, "Is this seat taken?"

He replied, "No, no, sit down, son." I sat down facing him. My curiosity was aroused. I wondered why it was that the room was full of only black people. They were all well-dressed, a neat bunch of people with their neckties and all. Because of my curiosity I thought that I would like to ask him what this was all about, but I didn't want to do that for fear of being rude, and I wasn't sure of my English. I really do not remember my exact question, but I asked, "Who are all these people?"

He looked at me and said, "These are my boys."

It didn't mean anything to me. These are my boys! Naturally, my next logical question was, "Well, sir, who are you?"

The man was eating chicken, a drumstick, chewing on it as if he was playing a harmonica. When I asked him, "Well, sir, who are you?" he placed the drumstick on the plate, wiped his hands with the napkin, and extended his hand to me. I shook it, and he said, "I am Duke Ellington."

And I said, "I'm pleased to meet you, sir." I didn't have the slightest idea who Duke Ellington was. I said, "I am Kashpar," as if that meant something to him. We talked a little bit, but my curiosity was still unsatisfied. Who was Duke Ellington? He had said these were all his boys. I wanted to ask, "What do they do?" I didn't know how to engage him in conversation, and he kept on eating.

Pretty soon he said, "Son, where are you from?"

"I am from Jordan Valley."

"No, no, originally, where are you from?"

I was kind of afraid to tell him that I was from the Basque Country because so many times when I said that to the other GI's they didn't know where the Basque Country was. They had never heard about the Basques, so I ended up saying, "I am from the Basque Country which is in the north central part of Spain."

"Oh, sure," he said, "Oh, sure, a Spaniard." Then he proceeded to tell me how he had given concerts in Madrid, Barcelona, Valencia, Granada and all those Spanish cities. When he said he had given concerts, I knew he must be a band leader and the people that he referred to as "my boys" were members of his band. But I still was not sure because I had never heard of Duke Ellington. After the lunch I excused myself, we shook hands and I left the dining cat. I still didn't know who he was until I got to Jordan Valley and I talked to the girl whom I was corresponding with and told her about the incident. She told me who Duke Ellington was, a famous musician.

I did not know that the blacks and whites were segregated and that blacks, Hispanics and many other ethnic groups were subject to discrimination. We were not aware in the Basque Country that such distinctions existed in the U.S.A.; because of that ignorance I walked into the dining coach crowded with black men.

My furlough was for fourteen days and of these days at least four were spent in traveling, coming to Jordan Valley from Gilroy and returning to Gilroy at the end of the furlough. So I really had only about nine or ten days to spend, and most of that I spent in Boise. I spent only a few days in Jordan Valley. In Boise, I stayed at a Basque boarding house, named Delamar, and while I was there I had the opportunity to have a few dates with the young lady that I was corresponding with. I hated to go back, but when the time came, I had to. Again, I said goodbye to all my friends and to the girl that I was dating, and returned to Gilroy.

After I arrived there, the life was no different from before. Patrolling Highway #1 and doing a lot of guard duty in several places like Fort Funston and many other places over in Monterey Bay area where they had the batteries of coastal defense. One of the most important parts of our job was to give what was known as local protection to these batteries, that is, coastal artillery. In addition to that, as I have already pointed out, we patrolled the coast of California, usually along Highway #1. After I returned from this first furlough the correspondence between the girl that I mentioned and me was much more intense. Perhaps you could say that we were in love; I'm sure that we were, I know that I was.

One time our company organized a company party in Santa Clara, California. This particular night everybody got into their best clothes or uniform, neckties and all, but I did not go to the party. I wanted to stay in my quarters and write a letter to my girlfriend. About 11:00 o'clock or so I finished writing the letter and decided to go to the party just to see what was going on, listen to the music, and chat with my friends.

The function took place at the University of Santa Clara or the College of Santa Clara. The U.S. Government took over this college and we were housed in the dormitories of the college. The party took place in the college gymnasium. When I got in there, the music stopped (not because of me, it just stopped). I spotted my friends at the other end of the gymnasium. I decided to go over and talk with them. There were several couples on the floor waiting for the band to start again. As I was walking across the gymnasium, I came across one man from our platoon, talking with two girls. As I walked by, they started talking to me. I stopped and tried to converse with them.

While we were talking, the music started and one of the girls said to me, "Say, what about us dancing?"

"Sure, why not," I said.

We started dancing, and this man, a corporal, got really worked up and said "Listen, soldier, you are out of uniform." I thought he was kidding.

"What do you mean?" I said.

And he asked me, "Where is your necktie?"

Me, like a damn fool, answered, "It's over there hanging in the closet." He said, "Well, you are out of uniform."

I realized that he was serious. I asked him "What are you talking about?"

He said, "You are out of uniform."

"I didn't come here to dance," I told him. "I just came to listen to the music and chat with my friends."

"You are out of uniform," he said again. Since my English was so limited at the time, perhaps not as good as it is today, I couldn't argue with him. I got so mad, I told him, "You stupid SOB, come on outside and let's settle this."

"Come on, let's go," he said. The other G.I.'s came around and stopped us, which was probably lucky for both of us. I think I could have beaten him. He was quite a bit shorter than I was, but stocky with bow-legs. He was uglier than the Spanish Inquisition!

Then he said, "Soldier, you are going to report for K.P. tomorrow morning at 6:00 a.m. That is an order!"

I replied, "Corporal, you go to hell, I will not report for K.P. tomorrow morning!" After this incident, we were not on speaking terms!

After that, we fooled around a little bit longer. All the excitement was over with, so I decided to go back to my quarters. I should perhaps say that I *was* out of uniform. I was in my fatigue pants, G.I. boots and a T-shirt. Everybody else was in what they call "parade dress." Because of my limitations with English, I always thought that perhaps I could settle my disputes by physical involvement, and on occasions such as these, when I got excited or worked up, it was hard for me to talk. There was no way that I could argue with an idiot like him, so that is why I challenged him. On the way to my quarters, I went into our platoon's headquarters. There was our platoon sergeant, a tall, skinny staff sergeant named Sergeant Krueger.

I asked, "May I come in?"

"Sure, Private Kashpar, come on in." He asked me, "What can I do for you?"

"Sergeant, I just came to tell you that I was ordered to report to K.P. tomorrow morning at 6:00 a.m. by Corporal Stash, so I wanted to tell you that I will not report tomorrow morning at 6:00 a.m. or at any other time for K.P. This was a personal incident between Stash and me, not relating in any way to the Army, and that two-bit corporal is not going to make me report for K.P. at that hour or any other hour by pulling his rank on me. I just wanted to tell you that I am not going to report, regardless of the consequences that I might have to suffer, and that's all."

For a few seconds he looked at me. "Well, Private Kashpar, you don't have to report at all. We will discuss this at some other time as to the consequences that may be involved. So, relax, and go to bed."

"Thank you, Sergeant. Good night," I said, and left for my

quarters.

One other incident I remember well is the following: One time there was a regimental field meet in Redwood City, California. There the whole regiment participated in some sort of the athletic races, javelin throwing, and all aspects of sports. It just so happened that in one of the races, namely the half-mile, there was nobody to represent our Battalion. When the time came for that race, the fellows who were to participate were all warming up for the race but there was no one from my Battalion. Our company commander stood up and looked at the crowd. He was going to select somebody to run that race. He pointed his finger at me. I couldn't hear him because of the distance, so he made a motion for me to come to him. There is no alternative in the Army when a Captain or a Lieutenant asks you to do something, you are supposed to do it. I didn't know what he wanted, so I went over to him.

"I want you to run this race," he said. And I said, "What race?"

He told me, "This is a half-mile," and so forth and so on. "Well, sir . . . "

"Now, don't give me any arguments, you run." "Yes, sir."

And there I was with fatigues and heavy G.I. shoes and all these fellows that were getting ready for weeks for this race, some of them in real fancy shorts and running shoes with spikes, the works! I thought, "How can I compete with these guys who have been training for weeks for this occasion?" Our company didn't even know about it and no one had been training for it. They lined us up for the race, and here was poor old "Succor Creek Joe" with his G.I. shoes and fatigues against these guys who had been training for weeks, all prepared for the event, the right equipment, and all that sort of thing. The race started. I thought I was going to use my head. I knew I had to use my legs, too. We took off. I didn't know anything about races, other than that you were supposed to run like hell and beat everybody. I thought I was going to try to keep up with the lead man and towards the end of the line, I would beat him.

After we started out, a lieutenant with the teal fancy shorts and running shoes with spikes took the lead and I followed him. Once in a while I glanced back and thought I was father comfortable running next to him. When we approached the finish line, I planned to speed up and beat him. When we got within 100 yards of the finish line I tried to pick up speed, but I couldn't do it. The lieutenant was just a few feet in front of me, but I just couldn't pick up the speed with those heavy shoes. I felt, rather than saw, somebody coming close to me, and here he came with real short, fast steps; a short, little guy. He beat me, and he beat the lieutenant! He took first place, the lieutenant took second place, and I took third place. After going through the finish line, I couldn't stop. I took in cadence of a certain speed and went almost another half mile before I was able to stop. I attribute that to the heavy shoes. My legs were really sore for days and days. I didn't think it was too bad to be able to get third place with all those trained athletes, and I got some sort of a ribbon, a blue ribbon I think, and that was the end of our race.

13
Engagement

After our basic training, I was assigned, along with all the recruits from Oregon, to the 125th Infantry Regiment. The regiment at that time consisted of three battalions. Each battalion consisted of four companies. Our duty was to give local protection to the coastal defenses and patrol the West Coast all the way from San Francisco to Santa Barbara. The regiment's three battalions were in this manner; two of the battalions were on field duty and one remained in the rest quarters which was Palo Alto. The battalion remaining in the rest headquarters would be involved in intensive training in various aspects of field tactics.

On one particular occasion, the training we were getting was how to overcome the barbed wire entanglement. We had several lectures on this, but in order to get a demonstration we had to wait until dark. I was selected to give a demonstration on how to go across a barbed wire entanglement without causing any noise or sound. One evening, the officers of our battalion gathered us in a certain place where they had already installed a barbed wire entanglement. After dark, one of the lieutenants started to give us a lecture on how to overcome these obstructions when you face the enemy. While he was talking, my assignment was to go across this entanglement with full pack. While he was explaining the operation I was crossing the obstacles, and there were many of them because in addition to the barbed wire, the enemy would hang cans or bottles on the wire, and at the slightest agitation they produced noise, and the enemy's guns, mainly machine guns and rifles, were already zeroed in on the wire. Whether dark or daylight, whenever the enemy heard the sound they opened fire and it could produce scores, perhaps hundreds, of casualties. So the idea was to overcome the enemy without making any sound. I went through the obstacle without causing any noise to the other side. The lieutenant saw me because I was close to him, and he asked the battalion, "Now, did you hear any noise?"

Almost unanimously, the battalion said, "No."

He said, "Well, I wanted to tell you that someone crossed this obstacle while I was talking to you. Then he commanded a bunch of jeeps and trucks that were set up around there for the demonstration to turn on their lights. Everything was lit, and there I was, standing up. The lieutenant said, "Come up, come up, Private Kashpar." I did, and he explained to the battalion that I was able to cross the obstacle without making any noise. The guys in the battalion applauded me. I thought that was one of the greatest things! I am sure that it was a good lesson to them, something that perhaps would save many of their lives when they went overseas.

While performing our duties while I was stationed at the College of Santa Clara, I received a letter from the girl that I was corresponding with, saying that within two or three days she was going to be in California in a town named El Cerrito. She asked if I could go over there to meet her. I was so glad, but I was in trouble. A guy from Ontario, Oregon, and I had applied for a pass one evening and our request was rejected. We really didn't care too much because we thought we were going to go out anyway, without a pass. That means AWOL. That night, our company decided to have a bed check. When we get a pass we get it from 6:00 p.m. to midnight, and after midnight they check our beds. The corporal on guard checks the quarters and turns in the names of those that are not in their corresponding beds by midnight. We were turned in as being "absent without leave," and both of us were confined to quarters. That means that for a certain period we couldn't even apply for a pass and whether we applied or not, it would not be granted. The only places that you can go are just around the premises where you are stationed and the PX. The girl was coming and naturally I wanted to see her. I went to see the company's master sergeant. I asked him for a pass, which he denied. I thought maybe I would go over his head and go to see the company commander. Normally we had to have the permission of the master sergeant and I knew that if I asked him he would not give it to me, so I went over his head to the company commander. I told the company commander the circumstances, how I was corresponding with this girl, she had asked me if I could see her but the master sergeant would not even consider letting me go and the reason I had come to him was to see if I could have a 24-hour pass.

The officer, Captain Lutz, was a real good soldier. He made some kind of excuses and some faces and I think he was trying to impress upon me that what I did was wrong. Finally, he said, "Well, I cannot grant you a 24-hour pass, but I will grant you a 6-hout pass." I knew that I couldn't go to El Cerrito and return after seeing her in six hours because El Cerrito was perhaps 100 miles. I didn't have the money to go by bus so I had to hitchhike. I really didn't care how long the pass was good for, all I wanted was to get a pass to get out of that place legally. Once I got out, I didn't give a damn what happened, or how long it took for me to get back. He called the company headquarters and ordered Sergeant Hensley to give me a 6-hour pass. I got the pass and started hitchhiking. I didn't have too much trouble getting into San Francisco. I crossed the bay and hitchhiked to El Cerrito. I found the place, but nobody was home. I found a note on the door saying, "Sorry Kashpar, we went to San Francisco to see and hear one of the most famous band leaders in the United States of America." (It was Jimmy Dorsey.)

I was so disappointed, all this trouble, and she didn't even wait for me. I had some paper so I wrote a note. I remember, while I was looking for that place that I saw on the main street of El Cerrito the name of a canteen or tavern named "Top Hat." I wrote her a note saying since she was not here, or something to that effect, I was going to go over and wait for her at the "Top Hat." "If you are here in time, you can come over." I walked to this place and ordered a beer. I hate beer! Even today, I don't like it, but they weren't serving anything else but beer until 5:00p.m.

Everyone that came into the bar said, "Give Joe a beer."

I couldn't figure out how they knew I was Joe. Then a guy

came in and said, "Give Mac a beer," and I drank from about 2:00 p.m. until about 5:00 p.m. At that time they started serving hard liquor. My favorite at that time was 7-up High. People kept on coming and saying, "Give Joe a drink" or "Give Mac a drink." I did not realize until later that every G.I. was known either as Joe or Mac. Drinking all the drinks that these people bought me, I got drunk! There I was, sort of feeling sorry for myself, I guess.

Later in the evening I felt someone jabbing a finger in my ribs. I looked back and saw a girl. I turned back to my drink and suddenly it dawned on me, "This is the girl I came here to see." I looked back again and said "What are you doing here?"

She replied, "What are you doing here?"

"What else could I do?" I said. "I came here to see you and you were not home, so I came to this place."

"The couple I am staying with are outside, come on, I want you to meet them," she said, and took hold of my hand. She led me to them and introduced me.

She said, "Well, let's all go and have dinner." Then she asked me, "Have you eaten anything, have you had your dinner?"

"No, I didn't eat anything."

"Well, come on, let's go eat."

She and her friends took me to someplace and we ate. There was some music there and we danced two or three dances. I was so happy. The couple went in the house and the girl and I stayed in the car and we talked about everything. I was sobered up by that time. We talked for a long time, and I realized that she needed to go in and go to bed.

I said, "I'd better go."

She asked, "Well, how are you going to go?"

"I'm going to walk to the main drag and hitchhike."

She said, "No, no, you can't do that, I don't want you to do that. I want you to take a bus and go to your destination."

I didn't have enough money to do that. She said, "O.K., let me take you to the bus depot." We walked to the bus depot and bought a ticket for Santa Clara. I say we, but in fact she did. She paid for the ticket, and I got on the bus. She and I waited for a little while until the bus came, we said goodbye, and that was the second time that we kissed. She was so beautiful!

When I got to Santa Clara about noon the following day,

I didn't care what happened. I changed my clothes and went to the field where a lieutenant was giving a lecture. While I was approaching the company he stopped talking and everybody was looking at me. It was an embarrassing moment, like they were saying to themselves, "Where had this guy been? What's he doing?" I was embarrassed, but not too concerned. I joined the group, found a place to sit down on the grass, and the lieutenant proceeded with his lecture. He didn't say anything to me. Nobody else did either. I listened to his lecture, but I don't remember what it was about. I don't think I understood anything. I was so happy about what took place the day before. While we were talking in the car, my girl told me, "I know now that you wrote these letters to me."

I asked, "what do you mean?"

"Well, your letters were so good, and knowing that you couldn't speak English too good, I didn't think that you were writing them. I thought that you had someone writing them for you."

I asked her, "How do you know now that it was me who wrote them?" I did write them, of course. I never did enlist anybody's help.

"Because, today, you came alone. I know that you didn't have any friends with you, and when I saw that note, I realized that this guy was writing these letters on his own, without anybody's help."

One thing that I would like to mention here is that I said several times that I did not have any money. When I started herding sheep, I think for a few months it was $40 a month, but not for very many months. Most of the time that I was herding sheep, the pay was $50 a month. After three or four years, it was up to $60 a month. And at the time that I quit to go to the Army, it was up to $80 a month, but I never received that amount as I went into the service before it went into effect.

In the army, a private at that time was receiving $21 per month. Out of his $21 they withheld insurance, which I wanted to have in case of death, for my mother. That cost $6.10 per month. Then for the laundry and dry cleaning our uniforms they withheld $2.90. So that left me only $12 per month. $12 a month after buying our cigarettes and from time to time a few candy bars in the PX, we didn't have any money to spend on passes or to cover the expenses that I have been talking about, such as the El Cerrito trip and bus fare.

Although my brother and I were in the Army and we both had our mother as a beneficiary on our G.I. insurance, we found out much later that our mother was not entitled to the benefits of the insurance because she was living in a foreign country. The same thing applied to benefits like monthly allotments for subsistence. Yet we were both American citizens and serving in the U.S. Army. Isn't that ridiculous? I think so.

After our encounter in El Cerrito, our correspondence became more intense. For my part, whenever I had a chance to write, which was almost every day, I wrote her, and she answered all my letters. Some-rimes we even talked about getting married someday and things of that sort. Yet, realizing that I was in the Army and sooner or later I was going to get shipped overseas, I thought that getting married perhaps was rather remote, but we felt good talking about it. Two or three months after this meeting with her, I received bad news from Jordan Valley. My uncle, who was also my godfather and the man for whom I had worked for six years, had died. I knew that he was in bad health for many months. When I got the word that he died, I asked for a furlough to attend his funeral. I didn't have any trouble obtaining the time off. It was something like a seven-day furlough, not very long, but long enough to go to Jordan Valley and attend his funeral. At that time it occurred to me that perhaps I should take something to the girl I was corresponding with. As I say, we talked about marriage sometimes, but I never did have the nerve to come out and propose marriage to her. I was always afraid that I might be rejected.

In Mexico there was a tribe of the native Mexicans, an Indian tribe known as Oaxaca Indians, and there is also a state of that name in Mexico. I read years ago about the customs of that tribe. If a boy was in love with a girl he gathered wild flowers and quietly placed them at the door of his love, then he hid behind a bush and waited to see what happened to the flowers. When the girl came out, if she picked up the flowers and took them in, then he knew that he was accepted. But if when she came out and kicked the flowers, then he knew that he was rejected. I decided to use that method.

I decided to buy an engagement ring and take it to her on this furlough and see if she accepted it. If she took the engagement ring, then

I'll know that I'm accepted. If she says that she doesn't want it, like the Indian girl, I will not be accepted.

I borrowed the money from a friend to buy an engagement ring. This friend was a Basque fellow (Jim Korta) that went with me into the Army from Jordan Valley and was killed in Italy! I truly loved him. After I got to Jordan Valley, I was very nervous and finally built up enough nerve and I told her, "I have something for you."

"Like what?" she said.

"Well, here it is." It was gift-wrapped, she opened it, and there it was, just a little teeny diamond. She was really happy. I knew from the expression on her face that I was accepted. That was really a happy moment for me. She asked me to put it on her finger, which I did. After a few days in Boise, and after attending the funeral in Jordan Valley, it was time for me to go back to camp.

From then on, we talked in our letters about getting married. We were really serious. We started talking about the dates and that sort of thing and when it was agreed that we were going to get married, I thought that it wasn't fair for me to marry her. As much as I wanted to, I decided that perhaps we shouldn't. The reason was that I knew that before long I was going to be shipped overseas and the chances for a person in the infantry to survive were very small. My feeling was that I wasn't going to make it. I was going to leave her a very young widow, or worse than that, I might be crippled. Anything could happen, anything. To impose such a burden, I didn't think it was fair. So I wrote to her often discouraging her from getting married, suggesting that we should wait until the war was over. She didn't want to wait.

"No," she said, "whatever happens, we've got to take it as it comes. Besides, we have decided, I think we should get married."

Finally, we made our decision to get married and on December 8, 1942, we were married in Redwood City, California, in Our Lady of Carmel Catholic Church. In this narrative, when

I was referring to the girl, I described her as the girl who "I was corresponding with."

The reader will recall how in one of the previous chapters I related that little incident of my lying down on top of the mountain and seeing a lonely star and making a wish. This is the sort of tradition in America, to make a wish and it will come true if you wish on one lonely star in the sky. I also said that I made that wish and the wish was for a certain girl to become my wife someday. That girl's name was Aurora.

Kashpar and Aurora the day they got married.

She was the girl that kissed me goodbye when I went into the Army. She was the girl that asked me if I would write to her. She was the one that sent me that dollar that I still have in my possession. She was the one that I went to see in El Cerrito and also the girl that accepted my ring of engagement. Aurora was the girl that became my wife.

On the day that I have stated, which was one year plus one day after the Pearl Harbor bombing, we were married. And strange coincidence, she and I were both born in Jordan Valley, in the same house, and in the same room. When my parents took me back to the Basque Country as a baby, Aurora's parents moved into our house from Birch Creek Ranch that her parents owned so the children could attend the school. A year after our family went to the Basque Country, Aurora was born in the same room where I was born.)

14
My Marriage to Aurora

When Aurora and I decided that we were going to get married, there was no way for me to come to Idaho from my Army camp, so we decided that she should come to California where I was. In order to get married, we had to have a blood test and after the blood test we had to wait three days before we could get married. That was the law in the State of California. We applied for a marriage license in Redwood City and had everything in order for the designated day.

That morning I was to get a three-day pass, or at least ask for a three-day pass, and hoped that I was going to get it, go to town and meet her, go to the church and get married. Well, it turned out to be that it was not that simple. First, the first sergeant refused to give me a three-day pass. I explained to him what the purpose of the pass was, but he said "No pass." I got so mad. Like I did once before, I decided to go see the company commander. I went to the barracks first, cussing.

Our platoon sergeant, Sergeant Milney asked me, "What is the matter with you?"

I told him that the master sergeant refused to give me a pass to get married.

"What? Why, that pot-bellied son-of-a-bitch! Let's go see him. You come with me," he said.

We went to the headquarters. This fellow, Sergeant Milney was a real nice guy, but he had a temper. I suppose this is what's known as the Irish temper. We went right into the headquarters where the master sergeant was.

"Sergeant Hensley," the platoon sergeant said, "what in the hell do you mean, not giving a pass to this man?" He went on telling the master sergeant how good a soldier I was and he didn't even finish what he had to say. The master sergeant was so afraid of this Irishman, that he called the clerk and asked him to write a three-day pass for me. Just like that.

I waited until I got the pass. I thanked Sergeant Milney for what he had done for me, we shook hands, and I was on my way to town to meet my girl.

I was already late, and I had a few other things to do, so I took a taxi in order to rush things up a little. I had to stop in town at the dry cleaners because two days before, on December 6th, we had marched in the military parade in San Francisco. It was a big affair, a spectacular parade, in honor of Madame Chiang Kai-Shek, wife of the Chinese chief of state or president. During the parade, it rained practically all day. We were marching four or five hours. It started in the place known as the Embarcadero and marched all the way to the northern part of San Francisco. My uniform shrunk. The sleeves of my blouse, which is the coat of the uniform, shrank between my hands and elbows and my pants between my ankles and knees. I stopped at the dry cleaners, and waited in the back room in my shorts while they pressed them at one of these places called "Press While You Wait." It was really embarrassing.

When I arrived at the hotel in Palo Alto where Aurora was staying and met her, she was mad!

She said, "Good thing you got here because I was thinking about taking the next bus to go back home." I told her the difficulties I had had, but she wasn't in any mood to understand. A little bit later on, she calmed down, and we went to Redwood City. We found the Catholic church and went to the rectory to see the priest. He told us that he couldn't marry us. I asked, "Why not, we are both Catholics." We wanted to be married in the Catholic church, but he said he couldn't because some regulations of the Catholic church prevented out marriage. In these days the regulation was based on the fact that there were so many girls marrying different guys on assumed names so that they could get their allotment when the men went overseas, and in order to prevent that we had to prove that Aurora had never been married and was not married to somebody else at present. I couldn't believe it, even from a priest, to say a thing like that about Aurora. It really griped me!

I said, "Well, we have a limited time, I only have a three-day pass, and we do want to get married through the church, but as long as it could be just as legal by being married by a Justice of the Peace, we are going to be married by the Justice of the Peace."

"No, don't do that!" the priest said.

"Well, what do you expect us to do? Wait until all these proofs are produced?" I knew that if I wasted a three-day pass waiting for these documents, I would never get another pass.

Finally the priest said, "Well, can you wait until, say, 3:00 p.m. this afternoon and in the meantime, I will talk to the Bishop and see if we could get permission from him?"

I hesitated, then finally decided, this wasn't too bad. This was about 10:00 or 11:00 in the morning, so for a few hours we could wait.

Aurora and I returned to the church at 3:00 p.m. sharp that afternoon in compliance with the priest's request. We met him at the rectory again and got the good news. He told us that he had talked with the Bishop and the Bishop gave him the permission to marry us under one condition, and the stipulation was rather a simple one. It was for us to get an affidavit from Aurora's parents that she had never been married, at that time she was not married to anybody, sign it, and send it to them. He trusted us and would marry us then, and then later on we could get that affidavit for him. That was simple enough. We were finally ready to get married. Then he asked us, "Where are your guests?"

"We don't have anybody, we are alone," I said. "We don't know anybody except our Army folks or fellow soldiers."

"But you mean you do not have even your witnesses, the people that will stand for you?"

"No, we don't have anybody. Is that necessary?" I asked.

"Well, okay, we'll arrange that," the priest said. This priest's name was Father Thompson. He grabbed the telephone and had two people, a couple of his parishioners, come to the church to stand up for us. The lady who came to stand up with

Aurora was Mrs. Powers and I do not remember the man's name. In a few minutes, these people showed up, and we went to the church. What a sad wedding! There we were, Kashpar and Aurora getting married with two complete strangers standing up for us. We went through the ceremony and when it was over, the Priest said, 'And now I declare you man and wife." It was so sad.

Mrs. Powers looked at me and said, almost crying, "May I kiss the bride?" She sensed the sadness in her.

"Sure," I said, and so she did. It occurred to me that when I went after Aurora, I didn't even take a carnation or a corsage for her. I didn't know these things were customary. She did. Aurora knew it and I think she was a little bit disappointed and hurt that I didn't give het any flowers. She was really a good sport and didn't say anything. I always remember that poor thing. These big weddings that people have nowadays, hundreds of guests and all that stuff and there we were in the church of Our Lady of Carmel, in Redwood City, so far away from our home, just the two of us. No guests, no reception, nothing. But the wedding was legal, so we walked out of the church as man and wife.

That night, Aurora and I had dinner in the dining room of the hotel, the President Hotel in Palo Alto, California. It was a chicken dinner, and the table was set with a candle. It was so neat. I was so excited the following day we were going to go for a day or two for our honeymoon to somewhere. I thought the appropriate place, in view of the limitations of time and money, would be Santa Cruz, over in the Monterey Bay. I was so excited that I bought two tickets for both of us to Santa Clara instead of Santa Cruz! How dumb! That was so stupid. There is nothing in Santa Clara. I don't know if there is anything spectacular there now, but at that time there was nothing. We were together no more than two weeks in Palo Alto after we got married. She thought that she had to return to Boise to take care of her business, which was a beauty shop in partnership with another lady. While in Palo Alto, in these two weeks, the things were pretty rough. During the weekdays, I had a pass to go out just about every night and we had a place in the Buena Vista Motel right along the Highway 101, a few miles south of Palo Alto. Every G.I., every soldier in our outfit applied for a pass on weekends and I never even attempted to because of the fact that I was getting a pass every day during the weekdays. I didn't want to interfere with these men during the weekend. The men really appreciated that so I did not have any interference during the weekdays from them. On weekends I went out anyway without a pass. I did not have any trouble. After a couple of weeks, Aurora came back to Boise, and from that point on being without her was very depressing, really sad. She returned to Boise and stayed until March. She realized that I would not be in the United States much longer and that I might be shipped overseas, so she decided to sell her share of the business. Her partner bought her out and she came to California to join me. I met her in San Luis Obispo. I will never forget when she came, that pretty little woman, so cute, coming out of the bus. She had so many things on her hands and arms—umbrella, purse, and I don't know what else. One thing that stands out in my mind was that she had a small, cheap radio that she bought from the Montgomery Ward catalog many years before. I had the arrangements made in San Luis Obispo in a hotel for us. I took her there. The place I was stationed at that time was Pismo Beach.

There was only one platoon in that place, Company C, the 125th Regiment, and we were manning an outpost along the beach of Pismo Beach. When I went to meet Aurora I had also made arrangements in one of the Pismo Beach motels for her to stay.

Pismo Beach wasn't much of a place, just a wide spot in the road. There was one motel, and it was the only place where I could make arrangements for my wife. We spent the night in San Luis Obispo, and the following day took her to Pismo Beach and this motel. After she arrived there, the lieutenant in charge of our platoon realized that my wife was in Pismo Beach. This lieutenant was a real nice guy.

He asked me, "Kashpar, why didn't you tell me that your wife was here? I didn't even know you were married."

I said, "Lieutenant, I didn't think it was necessary to tell you."

"O.K.," he said. "How would you like to take permanent K.P. duty so you can go home to be with your wife at nights and skip the guard duties?"

"That would be swell."

"O.K., then, I will arrange it." His name was Lieutenant Gera. So for about a month or six weeks, he assigned me to a steady K.P., no guard duty, and so I went into the camp, cleaning pots and pans and whatever in the K.P. In the evening from 6:00 until 6:00 or 7:00 o'clock in the morning, I got to be with my wife. After a month of this kind of life, my wife had to leave me again. Her father became seriously ill and her mother asked her if she could come home to help take care of her father. Her father had cancer and after a period of a couple months he passed away. Again, I asked for permission to go home to attend his funeral and I got only a three-day pass to attend it in Jordan Valley. It was very late at night when I reached Fort Funston on my return and it was one of the biggest surprises that I received when I got to the camp. When I approached the entrance of the camp I was challenged by the guard, which was a common occurrence.

"Halt! Who goes there?" said the guard.

"Kashpar."

"The guard asked, "What is the password?"

I recognized the guard's voice—I knew it was Parsons. I told him, "Parsons, I don't know the password, I have been gone for three days and the password has changed, it is a new password every day." Being absent for three days, I didn't have the slightest idea what it was. "What is the password?" he said again.

"Come on, Parsons, cut it out, you know who I am." I was not afraid of him aiming his rifle at me, because I knew that the rifle wasn't loaded. All the time that we were in California, we never had live ammunition when we stood guard, just blanks. I knew that Patsons didn't have live ammunition. Cut it out, Parsons, and let me in."

"O.K., Kashpar, come on in. Hey," he said, "you know there are congratulations in order."

"Oh, for what?" I asked.

"You."

"Me? What about?"

"Well," he said, "let me be the first one to congratulate you; you are a corporal now. You've been promoted." I was amazed over that. "You are kidding me," I said.

"No, I am not," he said. "You will find out," he said. The following day it was confirmed officially that I was a corporal. I had been nominated for corporal two or three times previously but was always rejected by the company commander who had the final say-so, because of my English. While I was absent, at my father-in-law's funeral, the matter came up again. There were seven candidates, including me, for one opening for corporal, and I was rejected again but the committee who determined who should be promoted was usually composed of noncommissioned officers of the company, and the committee thought that it was not fair for me to be rejected because of the language barrier. I had other capabilities that the committee thought should be taken into consideration in determining who should be promoted, and they felt I should not be rejected on the grounds that I spoke English with an accent.

The committee of non-commissioned officers decided that the company should hold elections to select the corporal and suggested to the company commander that the company should proceed with elections. He agreed, elections were held and of the seven candidates for that one vacancy, I was elected, probably setting a precedent in the U.S. Army! That is, electing a corporal rather than being appointed by the company commander, which is the proper procedure. That event made me feel very good and proud.

15
N.C.O. Training

About the time my wife went home because of her father's illness, I was sent by our company to what was known as the N.C.O. school. That is Non-Commissioned Officer's School, which was located in Gilroy, California. All non-commissioned officers of our regiment took that course which consisted of two months of field tactics such as compass reading, map reading, rifle marksmanship, and that sort of thing. It was a very intense training in military tactics. It was a very difficult course for me because of the language limitation.

First of all, when we arrived in Gilroy groups of fifty men were formed (a platoon consisted of fifty men). The officer in charge counted out fifty men for the platoon, all non-commissioned officers.

When our group came by him, he counted fifty of us, looked at the group and pointed his finger at me and said, "You, you'll be the acting platoon leader of this platoon. Move out!" he commanded. There wasn't anything that I could do, I couldn't protest.

The platoon that was formed of which I was supposed to be the leader consisted of all staff sergeants, master sergeants, and technical sergeants (except me who had just recently been promoted to corporal).

He said, "Move out," which means that you call the unit to attention, and then use the corresponding command either to the right flank or left column or whatever, forward, march, and take off. I was worried and very nervous and excited with all these people, many of whom were college graduates.

Later on I found out that there were two or three newspaper reporters from Los Angeles in our platoon, and I was in command of that platoon! It wasn't very easy, but I managed. I attended the classes, together with the other G.I.'s from Monday to Friday. Every Saturday morning we had tests. It was very hard for me as there were so many things that I didn't understand. But, surprisingly, I made it. My scores on these tests were anywhere from eighty to eighty-five which was well above passing, and although I was always the last to leave the classroom, particularly on Saturday tests, I made it. But, in the process I lost eight pounds. After eight weeks, we graduated.

One Saturday morning we had what was known as graduation exercises, and our regimental commander gave us our certificates, together with the "Good Conduct" medal. This same day my wife was to come back to California to join me and I did manage to meet her in San Francisco. From Gilroy we were transported back to our camp in Palo Alto by Army trucks and from there I went to San Francisco to the bus depot to meet her there. We spent the night in Belmont, and the following day went to Palo Alto and made arrangements for her to stay in one of the motels.

From here on, it was routine, again. We had to do our calisthenics, daily exercises and all that routine.

One day we were doing our exercises in Fort Funston which quite often consisted of sports like baseball, football and volleyball of which I knew nothing, but I liked to participate. I broke my leg. I didn't think it was going to be too bad so I didn't do anything about it. The following day, I couldn't walk. My left ankle was badly swollen.

I went to the medics and was told, "You have to go to the hospital."

I was taken to the hospital in San Francisco's Fort Baker. This place is right underneath the north end of the Golden Gate Bridge. There, after the examination, the x-rays showed that my left ankle was fractured. They put it in a cast and I was confined to the hospital. I let Aurora know what happened.

All this time poor Aurora came to see me whenever she

could, maybe two or three times a week. That was very difficult for her as she had to take a bus from Palo Alto to San Francisco's Market Street, transfer from one bus to another to come to Sausalito, and then from Sausalito she walked to the hospital. She had to walk downhill to where I was, but then when she was ready to go home she had to climb that steep hill to catch the bus to San Francisco and in Frisco transfer to Palo Alto.

While I was confined to the hospital, our regiment received orders to go overseas. We never did find out for sure just where overseas, some thought to Europe, others thought to Alaska. Nevertheless, the regiment got orders to move out. Our company commander, the man that I have already mentioned, Captain Paul Lutz, sent in a request to the doctor at the hospital in Fort Baker where I was confined, stating that the regiment was going overseas and asking for my release from the hospital. I saw part of the letter, "... I want this man to go wherever I am going." The doctor or the officials of the hospital granted his request and they sent me back to the company with a cast on.

The day I was discharged from the hospital we were riding from Fort Baket to Fort Ord (at that time our regiment was at Ft. Ord waiting to be shipped out), and while we were traveling in the ambulance (we were three G.I.'s, the driver, and a doctor, a Captain "Somebody") one of the G.I.'s asked the doctor, "Say, Captain, how come this man is going back to duty with the cast on?"

"Cast on?" the captain replied.

The G.I. said, "Look at him."

The captain did, and he was embarrassed! When he saw the cast on my leg, he got red-faced.

They had granted the company commander's request for me to be released to the company so I could go overseas with the cast on, and this doctor, who was in charge of my ward, didn't know that I had the cast on. We got to Fort Ord, and the man was so embarrassed he never took me to where my company was. Instead, he delivered the other two men and left me someplace on the base, where I didn't have the slightest idea where I was or where my company was. There I was, limping, with a cast on, and was about to start asking questions, "Where was the 125th Infantry Regiment?"

A G.I. came by in a jeep and saw me with a cast barely able to walk. He stopped and asked me, "Where do you want to go, soldier?"

I told him "125th Infantry Headquarters."

"I know where that is. Hop in."

I climbed right in and he took me to our company's headquarters.

My wife was staying at Palo Alto in that apartment that we had rented. I notified her by telephone so that she knew that I was in Fort Ord. It was a real mess at Fort Ord. To my surprise, the company commander requested that I return to the company with the cast on my leg, yet he wouldn't grant me a pass because of the cast. I went out without a pass just about every night, but I never felt comfortable about it.

One afternoon, I decided to go to the medics, that is the infirmary, to check my cast and remove it, if possible, so I could have access to passes like everybody else. It was impossible to get even close to the medics for the place was polluted with a bunch of "gold bricks." Many realizing that we were going to be going overseas were trying to find some kind of excuse for not going. I knew that I probably would have to wait hours before I got to the medics, so I decided to go back to my quarters. I was so mad, I cussed in English until I ran out of English cuss words and then probably continued cussing in Spanish until I ran out of Spanish cuss words and then in Basque.

When I returned to my quarters there was only one man lying on his cot and he heard me cuss and he asked me "What is the matter with you?"

I looked at him, and who should it be! It was Corporal Stash, the man that I had had that incident in the Santa Clara Dance Hall. Since that happened we had not been on speaking terms with each other. I told him the circumstances about all these gold bricks trying to stay away from going overseas and that I wanted to remove this damned cast and that because of it I couldn't get a pass to go out.

He said, "Why hell, I know how to take that cast off."

"You do?"

"Sure, I do. Would you like me to take it off from your leg?" "I sure would," I said. "Okay." he said.

Kashpar at the Non-Commissioned Officer's School in Gilroy, California.

"Relax, sit down on your cot and I will be right back." He went to the kitchen, got a glass full of vinegar and came to my cot with that glass of vinegar, a hatchet and a bayonet.

"Now, just don't get nervous, I'll take care of it," he started out. With a hatchet he made a cut in both sides of my leg's cast, just a light cut, then he poured the vinegar on the cast, and with the bayonet he scraped carefully so he didn't reach the flesh on my leg, poured more vinegar, and more scraping with the bayonet and in about 15 minutes he got that thing off. It felt good. I stood up, but I couldn't walk, because after something like six weeks with that cast on my leg, the leg was so weak that I couldn't stand on it.

"Sit down, I know how to take care of that," he said. "I'll be right back."

"What are you going to do?"

"You need a bandage and I'm going to get it."

He went to the PX and got one of those elastic bandages and wrapped my leg with it very tight. It felt good! I put my G.I. shoe on and I stood up. I was able to walk. I never stopped walking. I was so grateful to that guy. We made friends then, shook hands, and made apologies and all that kind of thing. I never did go to the medics and never had the x-rays taken which is a routine procedure when the cast is removed from your arm or leg or whatever, to see what the results of the break was. Without a cast, I was able to get passes just like anybody else.

As the time was approaching for us to leave, I'd noticed that my wife was not excited at all, everybody else seemed to be. I asked her something regarding it.

She said, "You're not going overseas."

I said, "What are you talking about?" We discussed it.

She said, "Something tells me that you're not going to go. "You just wait and see."

The day for us to leave came. We turned our mattresses in—turning the mattresses in was the best indication in the Army that you were going to move from one place to another. This was the time for us to go overseas. We climbed in the trucks in the convoy, started out, moved just a few feet and stopped. We waited for a long time and started moving again and stopped. I don't believe that we went over a hundred yards from the point of departure, when we stopped the second time and we waited over an hour and the order came, "Get off the trucks and draw your mattresses." Sure enough, our trip overseas was cancelled, just like Aurora said, so we didn't go, that time.

Another fellow, my Irish friend, Sergeant Milney and I went to Palo Alto with our wives and notified the owner of the apartment that we weren't renting any longer. We returned to Fort Ord. A bunch of fellows came out to the car where we stopped and somebody in the group said, "Guess what!" "What?" we asked.

"We are going back to Palo Alto tomorrow."

Sure enough we did leave for Palo Alto the following day and started hunting for an apartment. Aurora had to stay in a motel. After this incident, our regiment continued carrying on with a similar operation for several months. Then again, the rumors started among the men that we are about to go overseas. The way it happened is that all the privates from the regiment were shipped out somewhere on the West Coast. And from there, all of them went to the Pacific Theatre of War. We were left, the non-commissioned officers, from corporals on up to master sergeants and soon after we were shipped to Texas. That was the time that we left our wives. We left them in Gilroy. The wives were there when we boarded the train, watching and waving at us, and most of them were pregnant, including my wife. They were very sad waving at us and crying. We were in Texas approximately three months, and from there we were shipped to Maryland.

While in Texas we were told that we were going to have a furlough and it turned out to be that it was going to be only a seven-day furlough. Traveling by train, we needed probably all that time just to travel. In my case, to come all the way from Texas to Idaho and back, it would have taken at least six days. I was pretty disappointed. In view of these circumstances, I couldn't take the furlough.

From Texas we were shipped to Maryland. We were in Fort Mead in Maryland for a while before we were shipped to the marshalling area which was Camp Miles Standish in Massachusetts. There are a couple of incidents that may be of interest that I would like to relate, things that happened in Texas, Ford Mead, and Camp Miles Standish when we were getting ready to be shipped out overseas to the European Theatre of War.

In Texas we were near a town called Texarkana. The name of the base where we were was Camp Maxi. We were all non-commissioned officers and had to take our turns at K.P. Non-commissioned officers normally were free of K.P. duties. I was a staff sergeant at the time and there were many other staff sergeants, so we took our turns. One morning when it was my turn I reported, and a mess sergeant, whose rank was also staff sergeant, assigned me to a job which was to clean up the tables for the other soldiers. I started working, and about a half an hour later he came and asked me to do something else. This "something else" was for me to serve the officers. I asked him, "Why?"

"Never mind, why. I want you to do what I say."

I realized what had happened. Another sergeant had reported late. This sergeant and the mess sergeant were "buddy-buddy," and the latecomer told the mess sergeant that he didn't want to serve the officers, that he wanted to do something else. The mess sergeant decided that his friend could do what I was doing and he would put me serving the officers.

I didn't like it so I told him. "Look, sergeant, I came here and reported on time. You gave me an assignment and that's what I am doing, and if you want me to continue doing that I will, but I will not serve the officers."

He got mad and so did I, but we didn't say too much. I ended up by saying, "If you don't want me to do what I am doing, I will not do anything else. I will go back to my barracks. O.K.?" He didn't have an alternative, and I continued on my first assignment.

Another incident, rather a humorous anecdote was, one day after a long 25-mile hike, we returned to the barracks, showered, and ate chow and I decided to go to a show. Nobody else wanted to go, so I went alone. On my way to the movies, I stopped at the PX! There was not a soul in there. I was the only customer. I went to the counter to get some cigarettes, for I was out of them and having a strong desire to have a smoke, at the counter the young lady asked me "What are you all going to have?"

I couldn't figure out what she meant by "you all." For the word "all" I had always associated with plural. I glanced from side-to-side and nobody was there. In my best English, I told her, "I would like to have a package of Phillip Morris cigarettes." Just like that, trying to enunciate the words just as clearly as I possibly could.

"O.K." she said, and went away. Pretty soon she came back with a pretty good-sized decanter of strawberry milk shake and parked it right in front of me. That had to be for me I figured.

I drank it, and resorted back to my old tricks and asked her, "How much?"

She told me the amount. By that time I knew how much that was, I gave her a dollar and she gave me the right change. I walked out of there with a very strong nicotine fit.

Rather than continue on my way to the show, I went back to the barracks and bummed some cigarettes from my buddies. I was learning a little about the history of America along with other things and heard from time-to-time this and the other about the Texans, and I came to the conclusion that Texas was not a part of the United States and maybe they spoke a different language.

One other time, a very comical thing happened in our barracks. One Sunday morning we were just lying on our bunks, waiting for the paperboy to come around like he usually did, and about 10:00 o'clock in the morning he came. He was a nice looking, young, about ten or 12-year-old black boy. He came in with an air of confidence and inquired, "Where are you all from?"

Somebody answered, "We are all from Michigan, this is a Michigan outfit."

The boy replied, "I knew you all were damned Yankees," and everybody burst out laughing, except me. I didn't know what that meant.

I asked, "What were they laughing at?" That was how I learned the difference between the Union and the Confederacy, about the American Civil War, and who the Yankees were. In the Basque Country the Yankees were everybody from the United States whether they were from the north, south, east or west.

The commander of our temporary company was Lieutenant Toby. A big group of recruits arrived for their training at this camp, and among all of the non-coms that were in our company, Lt. Toby selected me to go to the training center to train the recruits that arrived, so I moved from my barracks to the training center. I couldn't figure it out, why the lieutenant designated me when there were people with better qualifications because of the language bit. I didn't complain, I just went and did my job. I do remember one time, as I was giving a lecture to these young recruits from all parts of the United States, teaching them the functions of the M-1 rifle and everything pertaining to the Army, a major came by pretty close to where I was talking to the men. He slowed down and stopped and by looking at him I knew that he was listening to me—no doubt the way I spoke English attracted his attention and I wondered what this guy was thinking! "How could a guy who speaks like that train our soldiers?" That was my thought. The night before we were shipped out of Texas, we had a little party and I asked Lt. Toby, who was an ornery son-of-a-gun, "Lieutenant, why did you send me to that training center when there were a lot better qualified non-coms to do the job?" He said, "I just wanted to see your reaction. I wondered whether you would accept it or not." I told him, "Lieutenant, anything pertaining to the Army, you should know that I would never refuse and if I could not perform the job, I would be replaced." He laughed, and said "I figured that." We had a couple of drinks together and the party was over.

From Texas we were shipped to Fort Mead, Maryland. There, literally thousands of soldiers were getting ready to go overseas. The way it worked out was pretty much like in Gilroy's Non-Commissioned Officers' School. Groups of fifty were formed, consisting of four non-coms or sergeants and forty-six privates. The lieutenant, who was selecting his own company, was a Texan named Lieutenant Sherry. When our turn came, that I was included in, the platoon of fifty, he looked around and pointed his finger at me and said, "You will be the acting platoon sergeant." I really didn't like that, and I went to him and asked him or told him, "Lieutenant, I have been promoted to sergeant recently. There are a lot more experienced men that could perform this job better than I could." He wouldn't listen. "Listen, you'll do it." That was all he would say. There was nothing else for me to say. Again, I went as acting platoon sergeant with these men and believe me, I thought I was in a different country for these people were completely different from the men that I was used to being with. People from the west, I suppose. All these men, all forty-nine of them, my platoon were from New York, Pittsburgh and other parts of the east. They were so indifferent. By the time the companies were formed it was already getting dark, so everybody went to their barracks. They were scattered all over the place. My job the following day was to find them, make a roster of their names, their ranks, their serial numbers, and from there on take charge of the situation, and get them all together. We were not in Fort Mead too long. Soon we were sent to Camp Miles Standish where we went through a very intense training. The men were so indifferent! They didn't seem to care about anything. I could give them a command and they would completely ignore it. When we used to police the area—police is, I suppose, Army lingo meaning to clean up the area of cigarette butts and burned matches and clean the area of litter—I used to line up the platoon and go behind them to see that the area was clean. These fellows wouldn't touch anything, they thought they were so damned smart. I picked up practically everything that was on the ground in the area that pertained to our platoon, rather than tell them anything, I just picked the stuff up. They wouldn't pay any attention to my commands. One time, when we were in what in the Army is known as a "close-order drill," they were very unruly, as always. They did pretty much what they wanted.

If I gave a command of right-flank they might take the left flank. I figured well, I'm not going to be with these guys too long so I wasn't going to do too much about it until I heard one of these bastards say, I'll be goddamned if I'm going to pay any attention to this foreigner's orders."

That got me, really. I commanded: "Platoon, halt." I was really mad, and my morale was so low at the time, for I knew that my wife was expecting a child and chances were that I might never see her and my child. I didn't have a chance to go see her because of a short furlough, and this idiot thought that they were going to go overseas and that I was just one of the guys on that cadre to train them, then put them on a ship and send them overseas. I stopped the platoon, asked the non-coms to fall out, and told them everything that I knew in English terms of cussing.

I started by saying, "You guys think you are so much better men in I am because you speak better English than I do. Well, I don't speak English very well, but there are other languages, more than one, that I speak and just because you speak English better than I do—that makes you better men than I am? I challenge any one of you to come out and fight and I will not take advantage of my stripes." I had staff sergeant stripes, I removed my shirt and I knew very well that I could take care of anyone in that bunch (I was 6' 1", weighed 182 pounds stripped, and was in perfect physical condition). Nobody stepped forward.

I said, "That figures. You are nothing but a bunch of chicken whatchamacallits, sons-of-a whatchamacallits. S.O.B. There are forty-six of you and not one of you has the guts to step forward and fight me. It is really sad to think that I have to go overseas with you yellow bastards to fight the Germans."

Then I said, "All right, now we are going to do the close-order drill." This was the break time, the customary ten minutes at the end of an hour. "We are going to do it, and we are going to do it right."

"Now one final thing, I will never touch another cigarette butt or a burned match. You guys are going to pick them up. If you don't you are not going to go out on a pass." I had them there, because as an acting platoon sergeant, whenever they requested a pass, they requested it from me and I had to initial their request. "You men are going to do it. Not me!"

I called them to attention, we started drilling, and I really gave them the works. All the other members of the company, of the other platoons, were watching, thinking maybe we were crazy drilling at the break period. The men did very good.

When we stopped, I dismissed them and over half of the men in the platoon came and congratulated me for giving them "hell." That was funny. They were not all that bad. There were probably some worse than the others, and maybe some of the guys were neat kids. Anyway, that straightened them up. I didn't have any trouble from then on, what I said was a command. I got along good with them.

16
Departure

After about a two week stay at Camp Miles Standish, we were shipped overseas. We were transported by trucks to Boston Bay and boarded the ship there. The following day, early in the morning, we left the port and began our way to Europe. After we came out of port and quite a distance from land, we began to notice other ships. It was a well-organized expedition. There was a time in our travel that we were able to count as many as 42 ships from the deck of the ship where I was. That included our Navy ships that were escorting us. It was interesting. Since we were traveling east, the whole convoy turned north sometimes and traveled in that direction seven minutes and then east again, then south, back to east. This was supposed to be to avoid a submarine attack. The Atlantic at that time was polluted with German U-boats. We were told that it took a submarine seven minutes to get into position to fire a torpedo, so the idea of traveling in a zigzag pattern was to avoid a submarine attack.

It took us twelve days to reach our destination, which was Liverpool. I have no idea how many people were aboard that ship, but it was pretty crowded. The conditions were very bad. We knew that that was to be expected under the circumstances. The food was bad, and bathing facilities were practically non-existent. I think the few showers that were provided for so many people, were salt water. Even our mess kit that we used to eat out of, we had to wash in salt water. The cots were from about a foot apart starting from the floor to the ceiling, five cots, very close to one another. I was lucky that I was assigned to one of the top cots. They were not cots, actually, they were just something like hammocks, and it wasn't very easy to climb up there, either. I was glad that I had the top one because, surprisingly, the number of G.I.'s that got seasick was large. And you know what the result of sea sickness is. For that reason, I didn't want to take one of the lower hammocks, but on top, with the slightest provocation, if I raised my head I hit the ceiling with my forehead. Boom! I spent most of the time reading novels. My favorite ones at that time were Perry Mason mysteries. We did have one thing. Every day there was a ration of candy, that is, each day we could buy one or two candy bars, and we took advantage of that because, actually, we were hungry and we skipped the chow and lived on candy because the chow was so bad.

We disembarked in Liverpool and were herded to a train, which was waiting for us, to take us to a city known as Norwich, where there was an Army camp, and all the soldiers in the camp were Americans. From Liverpool to Norwich we traveled during the night and arrived in our destination early the following morning. First thing, after we arrived, we were given another physical exam. Just about everywhere we went they gave us a physical exam. On this last examination, the doctors found one of our men had contracted mumps and right away we were quarantined, confined to quarters and were not allowed to go anyplace for 28 days. We were exactly one month in Norwich and for twenty-eight days we were confined to quarters! From there we were shipped again to one of the marshalling areas in the southern tip of England. I'm not sure which port it was. It could have been Southampton. Incidentally, the invasion of Normandy took place while we were at Norwich. In the marshalling area we were issued invasion money and live ammunition for the first time since I was in the Army, except at the firing range for training. Then we knew that this was the "real McCoy," as G.I.s used to say. We were in the marshalling area a few days because our departure to France was delayed due to a storm. I remember distinctly that the ship we embarked on was a Canadian ship.

Kashpar in an intense sixty millimeter mortar training that was his specialty.

It took only a matter of hours to cross the Channel. I'm not sure which one of these famous beaches we landed on, whether it was Omaha or Utah Beach. However, looking at the map and analyzing as to the location of the outfit I was assigned to, I think it was Utah Beach. We landed D-Day plus thirteen. We approached the land in the ships, just as close as we possibly could, then we climbed down from the ships to the landing barges on the rope ladders, then on to the beach. The sea was so rough that at least half of the men that were in the landing barges got sea-sick. What a mess! They threw up all over and when we hit the sand the front part of the landing barge, the gate came down and we got out. The depth of the water was almost to our necks. We walked through the water without full packs, trying to keep our loaded rifles dry above our heads and we made it. There was wave after wave of G.I.s coming, not only from our ship where we crossed the Channel, but to me it seemed like from hundreds of other ships. The enemy wasn't too far from where we landed and these tough G.I.s who landed there on D-Day were not only holding but pushing forward, slowly but surely. We climbed a very sharp, steep hill from the beach and could almost see the smoke of both, our own troops, as well as the enemy, shooting at each other. We walked between three or four miles behind our troops that were on the front line. These were the famous hedgerows. The moment we arrived on top we were under fire, that is, artillery fire, so we dug out along the hedgerows and waited there to be assigned to a certain unit. Actually we were replacements. We didn't belong to any particular unit. That is why we were known, excuse the phrase, as a "bastard outfit." About the time that we arrived at this place, the allies, Americans in this section, were fighting for the seaport of Cherbourg, so we waited for the outcome of this battle and to replace the casualties that the enemy inflicted on our units. We waited just a few days, and while we were waiting the conditions were very bad, especially the food. That was to be expected, but it was my luck that in three consecutive days that I drew my rations, I had along with the cheese and crackers (and whatever other items were in these C-Rations) I got lemonade powder for breakfast. I was so mad, that I wrote a nasty letter to my wife complaining about the conditions. Pretty soon, a lieutenant came around, trying to find out who wrote a certain letter. Poor guy couldn't pronounced my name.

Right away I knew that he was looking for me. He moved on and when he got close to me I asked him, "Lieutenant, are you looking for Kashpar? It is spelled such and such a way?"

"Yes, that's it."

"That's me."

"Oh." he said. He came to me and showed me the letter, which a lot of it had been censored. He was a very nice person. He said, "Well, I know how you feel. The conditions are bad, but this is war. We have to make the best of it. I do understand why you are so irritated, but do you want to write a letter like this to your wife? Do you want her to feel worse than she might be feeling now?"

I could see his point, "That's right, Sir." I said. Why should I tell Aurora that the conditions are so bad here? I asked the lieutenant, "Sir, instead of sending the letter like that, all chopped up, why don't you give it to me and I'll just tear it up and write another one to her."

He said, "O.K., I think that is a good idea." And then we stood up, shook hands, smiling, and in a military manner we saluted each other. He left and I wrote another letter to Aurora.

A day after that, we were assigned to our units. My assignment was, as well as many others, to the 79th Division, 313th Regiment, Battalion A, Company C, Fourth Platoon. The Company consisted of four platoons. There are, or were at that time, three rifle platoons and the fourth was known as the weapons platoon in a company. I was assigned to the weapons platoon as a 60 millimeter mortar squad leader. The weapons platoon consisted of one machine gun section (the section consisted of two 30-millimeter machine guns and one section of three 60-millimeter mortars), and that's the section that I was assigned to as one of the squad leaders. Each squad of mortars consisted of a squad leader, who was a sergeant, and then five privates, either private first-class or just plain privates of which one is the gunner, another one an assistant gunner, and three ammunition carriers. Therefore, the full mortar section consists of 3 squads of 6 men to the squad, a runner and section leader, a total of 20 men.

17
Assignment to the 79th Division

After the Americans took the city of Cherbourg in France, the whole thing had the atmosphere that the war was over with. Everybody was so happy and exuberant, not realizing that in reality that was just the beginning. After being assigned to our units, orders were to move.

Because of the success that the Americans had in Cherbourg and in that peninsula, the battle lines took a different shape, for the Germans were retreating, looking for a more advantageous place to set their line of defense. We had to move rather slowly. On July 4th of 1944, we were approaching the Germans, and General Omar Bradley issued an order that at noon on that day, as a celebration of the 4th of July, every soldier of every unit, whether it was a rifle, bazooka or short-range artillery, or long-range 155 Howitzers, was to fire one shot towards the enemy. At noon on that day, we did. Everybody fired a shot towards the Germans. From then on, we kept on moving. I was really proud that I was in that Army and this might sound silly, but I was not afraid at all. I was actually eager to meet the enemy, for as we were moving, every place I looked was our equipment—tanks, waiting for the enemy, in case of an attack, our artillery, anti-tank guns, just everything. I thought to myself, "Who could stop us with all this equipment that we have?" In addition to the equipment that I saw, I was eager to meet the Germans, because it was always so strong in my mind what the Legion Condor had done in the Basque Country. I thought 'this is going to give me a chance to see how tough these guys are with all this fighting equipment that we have and the Basques did not have. On July 6th, about two or three o'clock in the afternoon, as we were moving cautiously towards the firing line, the fireworks started. We hit the ground and started digging. After that encounter with the Germans and some of the things that I had seen happen that day, I wasn't sure whether I was that eager to meet them again. As we were digging foxholes, I felt something hit me on my forehead. It drew blood. I realized what it was. It was either a ricocheted bullet, or a piece of rock that hit me right on the forehead. I put my hand up on my forehead, I could feel blood, and I thought, 'These guys mean business.' I also noticed that there was a G.I. bringing two German prisoners back. The prisoners had their hands clasped at the back of their heads. There was an American officer sitting in the shade of a tree several yards away from them. When he saw these two prisoners, he stood up and went over to the G.I. They argued a little. The private and the lieutenant wrestled for the pistol the private was holding. Finally the lieutenant took the pistol away from the G.I. and the German prisoners knew right away what was going to happen. They started yelling, asking for mercy, I am sure. We were all paralyzed watching as this lieutenant killed both of them, just plain murder. Honest to God, I just couldn't believe it! It just so happened that this lieutenant who killed those Germans was a commander of a tank that the Germans knocked out earlier and killed all the crew in the tank, except him. He was so bitter, he was going to get even by killing somebody else. These two poor guys just wanted to quit and surrender. Nevertheless, the lieutenant thought he got his revenge and shot them to death. That was hard to believe. I didn't realize that we had that kind of men in our ranks.

We attacked the Germans, and after three or four hours of battle, they withdrew in retreat. We moved on to another area, slowly and quietly in a single line. As we were moving, there was a chaplain, a Catholic priest, with the "host" on his fingers, to give Communion to anybody that wanted it before we got engaged in battle again. We didn't have to have confession, we didn't have to kneel or remove our helmets to take the Communion and always received the absolution. Some guys, many of them non-Catholics, took the Communion because they felt the need. Since I grew up as a Catholic, I went and took Communion, said a prayer, and moved on. Soon after I took Communion, a German from one of the trees jumped to the ground. He was a sniper. These snipers would stay behind, often in the trees like this guy did, drink Schnapps, which is a liquor comparable to American whiskey, and as the American soldiers went by, shoot them in the back. The Americans did not have mercy for them at all. In that respect, I was in agreement. This German jumped and exclaimed, "Americans, Americans, Comrade." He wanted to surrender. It was too late. One of the G.I.s about seventy-five feet in front of me aimed his rifle at him and let him have it. Down he went. The column kept on moving in single file. Some of our men were still taking Communion, but we kept on moving, slowly. When we got real close to this German sniper, someone in front of me, eight or ten yards distance, yelled "Hey, the son-of-a-bitch is still alive!" Which he was, I could see him. Without asking any questions to anybody, the soldier aimed his rifle right between the German's eyes and shot him. He gave a few kicks, and that was it. We kept on moving, and soon engaged the enemy. It was an incredible battle. The weather was hot, shooting was intense. The Germans were throwing everything they had at us. While the battle was on, I noticed two German prisoners were brought in by an American soldier at the point of a bayonet. The two Germans had surrendered, and one of our men was bringing them back. The Germans again had their hands clasped in the back of their heads on their helmets. They were breathing heavily, I could hear their breathing. They were scared to death and they had reason to be. This probably was the most dangerous moment for the captured soldiers of both sides, because they came in from the battle, people were perhaps not thinking coherently. They were thinking of their friends who were killed. These two men were coming with the G.I. who brought them, his fixed bayonet almost touching the back of one of the guys. Just a few feet from where I was, our platoon leader, a lieutenant, stood up as the prisoners were coming by him and said "Goddamn, I'm going to get even for Sergeant Flagg." He had a carbine in his hands and emptied it on these two unfortunate Germans. The

Germans had realized what was coming and had started yelling pitifully. I didn't understand what they were saying. I just assumed that they were asking for mercy. This lieutenant did not have any mercy! He shot them right there on the sunken road. I could see them gasping for their last breath. At that time, or before I had witnessed these incidents, I had asked one guy, "What do you think of a war?" This man already had experience—I suppose along in Cherbourg, or wherever.

"Is it as bad as they say?" I asked.

"Well, no, it ain't so bad." This man was a Texan.

In our company, when we initiated that attack against the Germans, were 192 men. The Germans really gave us a beating. Our company was trapped, because the two companies—one on the left flank and the other on the right flank—withdrew and we were there in the middle, alone. The Germans moved to both flanks, and stopped us on our frontal attack and with their mortar fire on the back we were completely trapped. There was only one thing to do and that was to withdraw, and to withdraw we had to go through that mortar and artillery fire. That was the only solution, so we had orders finally to withdraw, so we did. From the 192 men that were on the attack, only 54 were left when we withdrew. There were casualties: dead, wounded, and prisoners. In that battle alone the Germans inflicted 138 casualties on us that afternoon, that is only in our company, and who knows how many more casualties were inflicted on the rest of our outfit. We retreated. As we were trying to retrieve some of our weapons, the G.I.s were going by me towards the rear. Among them was a sergeant that I knew. His name was Monelly. He was a tall, broad-shouldered, blond G.I. of Italian descent, always smiling.

As he went by me he said, "Kashpar, come on, shag-ass!"

I never knew what that expression meant, so I asked him, "Sergeant, what does that mean?"

He said, "Kashpar, that means everybody for himself."

And I asked him, "What about this equipment?"

"To hell with the equipment. There's nothing you can do about it. We'll retrieve it later, but right now, come on!" he said.

So, I followed him. Everybody was running just as fast as they could, including me. Then I realized how stupid it was to run with our packs and everything on when the Germans were firing at us, among other guns, their famous "88" mm, whose missile traveled 2880 feet per second.

I thought, "What's the sense in running, we can't run that fast!" I slowed down and started walking. Everybody was passing me as though

I were standing still. The Germans kept on shooting and we kept on running. We got to a place where there was a group of American officers with pistols in their hands stopping the G.I.s who were running in an absolute panic.

I remember one of the guys saying, "If the Germans knew how badly they beat us, they would have chased us to the beach with baseball bats." The officers who retreated, stopped us and reorganized us. The shooting ceased.

In the meantime, someone decided that we should go back to this place where we had been and recover some of the equipment we lost. This group was a sort of patrol, composed exclusively of non-coms. It was supposed to be sort of a volunteer effort. I volunteered to go with the others. We went quietly, seven or eight sergeants and corporals, but there were no Germans there. They were all gone. They had returned to their original positions, probably waiting for our counterattack. We saw lots of our buddies dead, among them was the lieutenant who shot the two Germans. I did not recognize him, but those who were with him for a much longer time did. He had one leg completely cut off. Evidently, it was an "88" direct hit and his face was badly distorted. I thought, maybe this was God's punishment to him for what he did.

A few days later, after our replacements arrived, we moved on again. And as we were marching towards the front for another confrontation, some G.I.s thought that they wanted to go to where the battle had taken place on July 6th. When they returned they told us that there were 11 American soldiers bayoneted to death. These, no doubt, were the wounded G.I.s that we were not able to bring back to safety and had to leave them there. When the Germans took that place, the area which was their objective and saw the two Germans killed, they knew that the Germans had not advanced that far and that they were not killed in battle, but were prisoners who surrendered. They knew that they were killed as prisoners by American soldiers, and in revenge they bayoneted these 11 of our men to death. We always were taught that once you captured a prisoner, just bring him back. Only on a few occasions were we given the orders, "No prisoners."

18
Fear of Never Returning

In the previous weeks, and particularly in this battle that I just had described in the previous chapter, I was almost sure that there was no chance for me to come out of this war alive, for what happened was only the beginning and we had a long way to go to defeat the Germans. In view of that, I started a frantic search to find out whether I became the father of a son or a daughter during the days that we were taking our replacements of the casualties that we received. I knew that my wife was due to have a child sometime in the last part of June, or perhaps the first part of July, but I wasn't receiving any letters from her. I thought that I would like to know how things were at home before I died. Then I thought it would be easier to die if I knew that I was a father of a child. I went to see the chaplain. I explained the situation to him and the only thing he could tell me was that he would try his best and that was all. There was no way he could find out if my wife had a child or not. I also went to see a representative of the Red Cross. There, too, I got the same answer. I knew that they would try, but their limitations were pretty much like my own. I could not find out in the three or four days that we were in this bivouac area, raking the replacements and getting ready again to move on to the front lines. After a few days, we moved on. I was very depressed. Maybe it was my fault for the fact that I wasn't getting any letters, but I doubt it because nobody else was getting any letters either. All my letters to her were always from "somewhere in England" instead of somewhere in France, because I did not want my wife to know that I was in the front lines. Perhaps that had something to do with me not receiving any letters. And this was kind of stupid on my part, also, because as I related a little bit earlier, that I wrote a letter from France that was strongly censored by the lieutenant and I wrote that letter stating "somewhere in England" and then described all about the situation in France. Well, my wife would have known that that kind of situation did not exist in England. After taking the necessary replacements and reorganizing, we moved on towards the front lines again. The battles in the hedgerows were bitter and tough. The German soldiers were really tough, well-equipped and well-disciplined soldiers. They fought well. They had the advantage on us because they could use the hedgerows as parapets to defend themselves, and we had to come out in the open to attack them. Therefore, we were easy targets for them. The enemy knew the route that we were going to take, which was only one way, and that is forward and in the open, and their weapons were already zeroed in on us. The minute they saw us moving, they opened fire and inflicted incredible casualties on us, but we kept on going and dislodged them from their defenses to the next hedgerow. The next day, the same thing happened again. There were some aspects that I did not approve of. We joined this unit as the replacements. We were not considered to be members of the unit that came to France, who had a certain pride that they belonged to the 79th Division 313th Regiment. Those of us who joined these outfits to replace the casualties they suffered were not considered to be members of these units. They always made a distinction of the old men, and when I say old men I do not mean to say old as in terms of age, but the old men who came with the unit to France. Almost in every case, when there was something that came up, like signing up the payroll or a certain recreation or things of that nature, the way it was announced was "signing the payroll for the old men," and we were left out. Maybe I should explain something in here, signing the payrolls and the recreations that I have mentioned, how that worked. A division consisted at that time of three regiments, two are engaged actively in the front lines, and the third regiment is always in reserve. Therefore, if the enemy should inflict large casualties or break through one of the regiments, the regiment in reserve replaces or supports the regiment in trouble, and these were the times when the regiment is in reserve had a chance to sign payroll and perhaps have some recreation and maybe even hot chow. I recall that on one of these occasions our regiment, the 313th Infantry was in reserve. There was some recreation for the soldiers, a movie, to exhibit in a certain place just around where we were. If I remember right, the title of the movie was "The Pinup Girl," and the main protagonist I believe was Wallace Beery. Personally, I couldn't care less, I never attended these things. These movies and this kind of entertainment never did build up my morale. I was too depressed wondering how things were at home. It was announced, "This afternoon at such and such a time there is going to be a movie shown in such and such a place," which was a great big French barn and only for the "old men!" That means the "new men" were excluded.

At about the same time, they announced: "Hear this," or something to that effect. "There will be from such and such time to such and such a time for the signing of the payroll for the old men."

So again, we were excluded, and still fighting with the same outfit, the same unit. While we were bivouacked in this certain area, it was one of the few times during the battle that we had a chance to have "hot chow." We were in our foxholes and someone beat some kind of a pan as a bell calling for chow.

And he yelled, "Come and get it, chow time, come and get it."

I came out of the foxhole, stretched my arms and I yelled just as loud as I possibly could, "Is that for everybody, or just for the old men?"

The G.I.s, the replacements, like me that came out of their foxholes getting ready to go to form the chow line laughed. They thought that was funny. I thought so too.

I looked around and I spotted a man looking at me. He was rather tall, with a red beard. He gave me a very dirty look. He was our company commander and he didn't like me to make a remark like that.

Kashpar

We went and had our chow and the next thing I knew, that afternoon I was reduced to private. From staff sergeant to private. I never knew the reason, but I suspected that the company commander, whose name I never did learn other than he was known as "Captain Dusty," that because of what I had said, decided "I'm going to show that whatchamacallit" and so he reduced me to private. It really didn't matter a heck of a lot whether you were a private or a lieutenant or whatever your rank may be, except for the pay. The reduction of pay didn't amount to much. Anyway, I was busted; but things happened so fast, the casualties were inflicted on us so fast, like the G.I.s used to say, they were promoting people to officers like hot cakes. In less than two weeks, I was a staff sergeant again. This Captain Dusty, whose recommendations were for me to be busted, didn't have time, that is the necessary documents didn't even have time to go through the regiment or battalion headquarters. They never did go through. I was never reduced in pay and I continued to be a staff sergeant. I was told, of course, to remove my ribbons, but I didn't have to, because overseas we never did have any ribbons on our arms because in our training we were always told that you should not have them. The lieutenants also, did not have their bars on their caps and their helmets because the enemy usually tried to spot and hit them first whenever they had a chance. So everybody was really equal. I never did lose anything.

19
Spectacular Breakthrough

After five weeks of struggling on the hedgerows, things began to happen pretty fast. On July 25th, I witnessed, along with the other G.I.s, perhaps one of the most spectacular events of the Second World War. This event was the American's breakthrough of St. Lo. That day literally hundreds, perhaps thousands of American planes bombed the enemy main line of resistance. I do not know the statistics on how many planes took part or for how long they bombed the area, but we watched our planes go over the enemy lines and drop their bombs where we could see, turn around, go back and wave after wave continuously return for hours and bomb the enemy. While watching this spectacle, out division was assigned to General Patton's 3fd Army. Up until that time we were part of the American 1st Army under General Omar Bradley's command. At the end of the bombing we were ordered to jump off and attack the enemy. Since our division was one of the closest to this area of bombardment, it was assigned to "spearhead" the attack. From the 79th division, our regiment, the 313th regiment, was assigned to "spearhead" and from the regiment our battalion was assigned to spearhead the attack. About 5:00 o'clock that afternoon we went to attack what was left of the Germans, but the only Germans that were there in the lines that we had bombed were the dead ones. Literally, we saw hundreds, perhaps thousands, of them dead. We kept on moving, thinking that maybe we would engage the enemy, but there was no enemy to be engaged close to us. We pushed forward until dark, and spent the night in the enemies' abandoned trenches. Early the following morning we started chasing the Germans. As a "spearhead" we were loaded on the trucks and chased them to the next town where they offered resistance. It was a town named Folgieres. On the outskirts of town, we came off the trucks and attacked it with fixed bayonets and drove the Germans out. After the enemy left, we climbed back on the trucks and again chased them to the next town which was a relatively big city named Laval. There we found strong resistance and engaged the enemy on the outskirts and fought it out for several hours. Slowly moving we broke the German resistance and were ordered to climb on the tanks. This was really spectacular. Just like something you see in the movies. We rode in the tanks, dispersed through different streets of the town and whenever there was the enemy, we shot at them from the tanks and ran them out of town. Once the first line of the resistance was broken, they did not offer too much resistance. They surrendered rather easily, or ran like hell. From there we moved on just as fast as the trucks could take us to the next town, which was the famous city of Le Mans. There, on the outskirts of Le Mans, we stopped and prepared to attack it the following day. But we received orders to move from the road to the woods for the French 2nd Armored Division was coming and they requested the honor of taking the town of Le Mans. Their request was granted by the American authorities (I suppose Patton, as this division was part of his Army). The commander of it was the famous General Leclerc. In the morning, early, we heard the tanks moving, slowly they dispersed, taking their positions. Really something to watch. And in spite of what a lot of people think of the French, I have a deep respect for the French, they were good fighters. Very good soldiers. They moved forward and engaged the enemy and broke their lines in no time. They went all through the town and we followed them on foot. It was a spectacular thing to see. The French people were such hospitable people. They came out crying, "Vive L'Americain, Vive L'Americain!" and they brought bottles of cognac, wine, and anything that they had and shared it with the G.I.s. On the outskirts of this town we were ordered to turn north to a town named Falaise. This maneuver was designed to prevent the retreat of the Germans and their escape from the pocket it was developing that later on was known as the Falaise Gap. The intention was to trap them there, so we headed north, to cut their retreat. We took town after town with very little resistance, Argentan and some others including Falaise, so we set them in the Falaise Gap, trapping in the neighborhood of 200,000 German soldiers. Some of them managed to escape, but the greatest majority of them were made prisoners. We were at this position only a few days. When the Germans were rounded up we were ordered to move east, directly towards Paris. One little incident that I would like to relate, was while we were moving east. I noticed that my fountain pen was missing, that I did not have it in my pocket. This was about three or four miles from Falaise when I realized it when we were marching. We used to carry writing material in our helmets, between the helmet shell and the helmet lining to keep it dry. I had this pen that was a present from my wife, about the time that we were married. This pen wrote many, many letters, not only mine, but also those of my buddies. And when I realized that I did not have it on me, I knew what happened. I left it where I wrote my last letter to her in a foxhole near Falaise. I decided to go back because it meant so much to me. I told some of the non-coms what had happened and that I was going to go back and see if I could find it and then I would return. I walked three or four miles and found my foxhole, and sure enough, the fountain pen was there. I picked it up and returned to my outfit. This pen, I still have it with me. It's all full of teeth marks because when I would start writing a letter to her, I usually held it in my mouth and unscrewed it and then write a letter and then put it back, screw it, and then put it back in my pocket. This pen and a watch that she gave to me as presents when we were in Palo Alto right after we were married I still have them with me. The watch isn't running and the pen hasn't been writing for many years, but because of the sentimental value I have them both with me. We continued on our march toward the east and we encountered a few pockets of resistance by the enemy. They were really intelligent soldiers. The idea was to hold our own column, maybe with a platoon of Germans, while the rest of their units move on back to better positions of defense. One of these occasions, when we were riding in a convoy, we saw American planes returning from their mission. These planes were escorted by four P-38 planes. They came in diamond formation. At the same time there were twenty plus German planes returning to their bases from their mission of bombing the Allied lines. Out of these four P-38 planes, two of them broke away from the formation and chased the twenty or more German planes. But it was clear to us, that the Germans were not too eager to engage them in a dog fight. They just kept on going and avoided our planes and in their attempt to get away from our planes, one of the Germans was stranded. That is, it was left behind. All the others took off and with the two Americans decided to return escorting our bombers. One of our planes spotted the German way behind from the others and he gave chase. It was incredible. These P-38's were very fast planes, and he caught up with the German from behind. When he got close to it we could see our plane almost come to a standstill just as if he applied brakes. What happened is, our pilot, when he opened fire on the German, the power of all the machine guns or whatever the P-38's were firing, slowed down our plane as if it came to a standstill and we saw the German burst on fire and the American turned around and went to join his crew. As the German plane was coming down, we watched to see if anyone bailed out, but nobody did. There were many occasions, similar to that one, that we had seen on the front lines. One other time, we were again on a convoy moving and another formation of German planes came after us. We had no air escort. They dropped a few bombs on us and strafed us with their machine guns. When we realized what was happening, we jumped off the trucks and hit the ground just as far from the road as we could and lay there. The enemy planes made several passes, mostly firing machine guns, and then they left after inflicting some casualties on us. When we realized that we were relatively safe, we started towards our trucks to resume our moving. There were many wounded and dead G.I.s. Among the dead I recognized one that was Sergeant Monelly. I talked a little bit about him before. This was the man that told me, "Kashpar, shag-ass." And I didn't know what that meant. There he was, dead. It was so sad that a man like him with that indelible smile on his face all the time, no matter the danger, should die. He was such a gentle person. I always said a prayer for every G.I. that I saw dead and I saw a lot of them. I always recited the Lord's

Prayer in Basque, because I never learned it in English. That was sort of a policy that I adopted on my own. I crossed his hands. I placed my hand on his forehead and thought, 'What an injustice. Why should a man like him and thousands of others like him be killed on both sides?' I left him there hoping that maybe they would ship his body to the United States so that his loved ones at least could place some flowers on his grave on occasions like Memorial Day. I climbed on the truck and we kept on moving. On one occasion, where we were chasing the enemy, we stopped in one little town. We had a chance to mingle around in town for an hour or so. Everybody went to town. As I was walking, I noticed another G.I. walking in the opposite direction, towards me. He was a tall, dark man. From a distance I noticed that he was looking at me. When we came within speaking distance, he said in Spanish to me, "Hola, Amigo." That means "Hello there, friend." He stretched out his hand and we shook hands. We talked in Spanish for a few minutes. He wanted to know where I was from.

I told him and then I inquired the same thing of him. "Where are you from?"

This fellow was from Argentina. He came to the United States illegally and joined the American Army, hoping to gain his American citizenship. The odd thing about this Argentinean was that he sensed that I spoke Spanish. Perhaps because of my complexion. Really neat guy, with black, straight hair. He was carrying his weapon on a sling and his helmet in his hands. We were talking a little bit exchanging our backgrounds. After a short visit, we departed company.

Soon after we were on the move again, and after a few miles we got into a big meadow and stopped to bivouac. Soon after that we dug our foxholes and got ready to spend the night there, two German planes came and strafed us unmercifully. The biggest weapon we had against the planes at that place was 50-caliber machine guns. When they made the first pass, everybody jumped in the foxholes. Soon some officers started yelling, "Shoot at the bastards." When they came in the second time, there were quite a few men shooting at them. And when they came for the third pass, all of us were shooting at them, and I don't mean from our foxholes either, everybody was out in the open. We had a little bit of that kind of training in the United

States, how to shoot at the airplanes. You didn't aim directly at them, just lay a curtain of fire in the path that the planes might be likely to travel. So in this manner we shot at them from both sides. At the beginning of the third pass, we waited for them and as they came we started shooting. In the fourth or fifth pass, we got one of the planes. Everybody let out a yell when we set the plane on fire. These Germans were so close to us that we could even see their teeth when they smiled. They were enjoying it because they knew that we didn't have any anti-aircraft or weapons to fight them, they felt very cocky. Everybody was shooting whatever they had. Some of them were shooting their 45-caliber pistols. The second plane never did show up after we got the first one. The following day, we went to the road marching forward and saw the destroyed plane and part of the dead pilot. The G.I.s partially buried him in a shallow grave; they left one of his legs sticking out of the grave. We moved on and got into an area where, for the first time in a long time, we were going to have a chance to relax, clean up a little bit, shave and sleep with our shoes off.

20
A Needed Rest That Did Not Come

By this time I was promoted to section leader. The platoon sergeant, Sgt. Roberts, was killed. The machine gun section leader Charley was promoted to platoon sergeant and I was promoted to mortar section leader.

I would like to explain the functions of the 60mm mortars section and its section Leader. Whenever the infantry company engaged the enemy, the mortar section stops and finds the most advantageous positions to use its weapons the most efficient way. The section leader continues on with the riflemen and digs in wherever the riflemen dig in. From there he issues five orders; (1) he spots the likely targets (usually an enemy's machine gun nest or a mortar nest); (2) once he spots the target he issues the fire order (this is accomplished as follows: the runner stretches the wire from the position of the mortars to the section leader. They attach the field phones to the wire at both ends. One of the mortar squads, usually the second squad which is in the center of the three squads, receives the fire order from the section leader. The order goes like this: "Direction, so many degrees. Range, so many yards" . . . , and the squad leader of the center squad repeats the order aloud so the other two squads could hear and the three weapons set their mortars aiming at the target identically the same way); (3) after setting the mortars according to the fire order from the section leader, the leader orders: "Fire one round." (Only the mortar in the center fires one round), and he observes the burst of the shell with his field glasses as to how close it was to the target. He then makes the necessary adjustments like: "half turn up or down for range, one fourth to the left or right for deflection" and after the proper adjustment, issues the order; (4) three rounds fire for effect. Of it could be 5 rounds. With such fire order there were nine rounds or 15 rounds of 60mm up in the air aimed at the selected target and was invariably a direct hit; (5) then the section leader spots another target and goes through the same procedure again. The standard equipment the mortar section leader carried, in addition to his weapon, was a compass to get the direction of the target and binoculars to spot the enemy's targets and observe the shell's burst or explosion in relation to the target to help him make the corresponding adjustments.

In this place where we bivouacked we were contemplating a rest, and have certain amenities such as a shave, a haircut, take a sponge bath by using cold water with our helmets as bathtubs, and mainly be able to sleep that night with our shoes off for the first time in many days, perhaps weeks. Sgt. Charley was a barber by trade from somewhere in the east, I believe from Rhode Island. It was decided that Sgt. Charley was going to give us a haircut, and in payment each man in the platoon was going to dig a few shovels full of dirt for his foxhole. Everybody dug their own and also finished digging one for Sgt. Bolera. We shaved, ate our rations, and after dark we were ready to go to sleep and get some rest. For some reason or another we thought we were in a particularly safe place and were going to have a good night's sleep without any interruptions. After dark we all lay down in our slit trenches, covered with our blanket and a raincoat just in case that it might rain. We were told that this was the rainiest year that the French had experienced in the past 85 years. Everything was quiet. Along about 10:00 p.m. there was a G.I. coming around and waking us up. "Up and at 'em." This was the standard expression of the American G.I.'s. We just wondered what was going on, but when we get an order, we just do not ask any questions. We just get up. We didn't sleep an hour. We put our shoes on. We didn't need to put anything else on, as we were fully dressed with the exception of our footwear. We moved out. We didn't know where we were going, but it turned out to be a very interesting move of historical significance. Instead of having the nice rest that we were anticipating, we were awakened and ordered to cross the Seine River. At the time we approached the river there was a terrific thunder and rain storm. We crossed the river that night holding each others' shoulders, that is, placing one hand on the shoulder of the man in front of you to avoid falling in the river. The patrol that scouted ahead of us stretched a white tape so the men leading us crossing the river knew where we were going. During the flashes of lightening was the only time we could see where we were going. We could see the river way down in the canyon. It was scary. Finally, we got on the other side of the river and kept on moving and stopped on the outskirts of a town named Mantes, about 20 miles north of Paris. We were exhausted. I do remember that even under those conditions I fell asleep, and so did many other G.I.s, in spite of the rain. At daylight we didn't know what to expect. We thought that perhaps we might have a chance to warm some instant coffee and eat a chunk of cheese and crackers for breakfast. Instead, we had orders about 9:00 a.m. to fix bayonets and to attack the town of Mantes. We were tired, sleepy and hungry, but with an order like that we felt no hunger nor fatigue and weren't sleepy at all. We got ready and attacked the town. We were all soaked and wet, and when the storm subsided and the sun came out, from the wet clothes of the G.I.'s the steam was coming out just like fog. We moved on to this town. We took the town without firing a shot for there were no Germans there. There was nobody there, except the French people who came out crying "Vive l'Americain" and they brought their schnapps, cognac, bread and whatever they had as usual saved during the war. They were very friendly and so good to us. As we were moving slowly and carefully into town, since we didn't know if there might be some pockets of resistance or snipers or some fanatic Nazis, we heard some commotion. People were coming down the street, like in a parade. We watched, wondering what it was, Germans? No, it was the town people, the so-called Maquis, the French freedom fighters. They brought along with them 8 or 10 girls with their heads shaved. They called them (the girls) the "collaborators." These were girls who were friendly with the Germans, and the French didn't like that. So when the Germans were gone, they rounded these girls up, shaved their heads and paraded them all over the town as traitors. Many of them were the lovers of the German soldiers, and, naturally, the French who were defeated by the Germans hated that. They didn't like their girls to chum around with the Germans, so the Frenchmen adopted this method to punish them. It was embarrassing to them. People threw things at them and insulted them. I have no idea what happened to them later on. I did feel sorry for them.

We moved on to high ground. We realized, at least I did, what was going on. We crossed the Seine River and we were to defend that position regardless of what. The Germans in their retreat had not crossed the Seine River yet. We beat them, and our regiment was 75 miles from our closest friendly troops. Our mission was to set up a line of defense across the Seine River and hold the Germans there until the Americans could build pontoon bridges, or whatever was necessary to get the troops and equipment across. After we crossed the river, the biggest weapon that our regiment had was the bazooka; however, we did have artillery across the river and air support. Our long-range 155 cannons and others were on the west side of the river. On the east side of the river, we were the only people (the 313th Regiment of the 79th Division). We were told that the Germans thought that those who crossed the Seine River were American paratroopers, for they did not realize that we could move so fast and cross the river so quickly. Shortly after we crossed the river we were told the enemy placed two divisions against our regiment. Our regiment could not move too far ahead after crossing the river, realizing that if we go too far our flanks would be vulnerable to their attack. The two German divisions, one a Panzer Division and the other one a conventional foot infantry division, were facing us just a day or two after we settled and dug in this place. The area was sort of a basin. From where we were it extended quite a ways east, a rather flat, beautiful country gradually going up to another range of mountains on the other side. That is where the Germans came from to face us and there we were waiting for them, expecting the attack anytime. When we set up our lines, our main line of defense, an outpost, was set within a mile in front of our main lines. This outpost was manned by about fifty men. These fifty or so men consisted of the weapons platoon, which was the machine gun section and 60 mm mortar section, of which I was in charge, and one platoon of riflemen. The purpose of the outpost was to feel the strength of the enemy when they attacked. This was almost like a suicidal mission. We were to test the strength of the enemy and from there the main line of defense would know what to expect. While in the outpost I noticed some activity in the enemy sector. I noticed a patrol of Germans coming toward our lines. I often stood guard just to give a break to the men of our section. As a section leader, I didn't have to stand guard, but I always did. This was in the daytime, and I was watching the Germans. I grabbed the phone and called headquarters and reported what I had seen and asked for instructions.

"What shall we do? Get them or take them prisoners if we can?"

"No." was the command. "If they are coming by, just keep an eye on them and don't shoot at them. Don't try to take them prisoners. Just let them go by and we'll take care of them. We like to take them alive to find out from them what's going on on the other side."

I called some of my buddies and two or three of us were watching their movement. The enemy patrol went by us and the G.I.s on the mainline captured them with no problem, and from them we learned that the Germans intended to launch an attack the following morning at daybreak. (This was the reason I felt it was so important to capture these people alive.)

We were told, "In the morning, at daybreak, be alert for the Germans will attack." We waited all night. It was a very bad night. It was raining all night. We were soaking wet. Water running all over. It was miserable.

I wish to make a brief observation regarding the crossing of the Seine River by the Americans under General Patton. I have read three versions of this remarkable feat; one by an Englishman who, in my opinion, did not give a proper credit to the Americans; another version by a German author which was nothing but an apology for not having sufficient equipment and ammunition to stop the Americans (what about the Belgians, Dutch, Norwegians, Basques, and others), and the third version was by an American author, in my opinion the most impartial version. All three of them mentioned that an American patrol crossed the Seine and found no sign of the enemy on the other side of it and the patrol reported their findings to the higher-ups who, in turn, realizing the significance of the finding reported immediately to General Patton's headquarters who ordered Major General I. T. Wyche, commander of the 79th Division, to cross the Seine immediately. "On August 19th, 1944, when the troops had already settled down for a night's rest, not too far from the river, General Wyche roused his men from their blankets, and in torrential rain the 313th Infantry Regiment crossed the river on foot over a weir that offered the only dry crossing in the area, each man holding onto the shoulder of the man in front to avoid falling into the river." (Quoted from "Breakout Drive to the Seine" by David Mason.)

I told the men in the section of which I was in charge to find a dry spot if they can and relax and see if they can get an hour or two of sleep and I'll stand guard. I was there alone standing guard, but I am sure my buddies were not able to sleep. After midnight I could hear the Germans issuing orders, but could not understand them. They were placing their tanks in position to attack in the morning. I could hear the tank commanders of the enemy howling orders, which is a normal procedure to place the armored unit in position for an attack, and towards morning the things quieted down. Obviously they were already in position to jump on us at daybreak, but at daybreak nothing happened. We waited for the attack, but no attack. No doubt that it was delayed because of bad weather. One thing about the Americans as good soldiers and tough fighters that they were, they lacked one thing, and that was discipline. We were just nothing but real ordinary guys in uniform, people who grew up in a democracy. They didn't believe in the nonsense of the "goose step" and that sort of thing. When the Germans didn't show up by 9:00 o'clock, everybody thought that they weren't coming so they started building fires to dry out and warm up their Nescafe, and that smoke gave our position away. As a result we endured an incredible artillery fire. We put the fires out and sweated out their barrage and waited for their attack.

About an hour later the rifle platoon Sgt. McConaghy, better known as Sgt. Mac, told me, "Kashpar, these guys aren't coming. Let's go on a reconnaissance." This was kind of a game with us, because if there was no activity and no movement in the front, they always formed some sort of a scout or patrol to go scouting to no man's land. Between the Germans and us there was a little town in that basin, so he thought we would go over there and see what it was all about. Three of us, Sgt. McConaghy, Lt. Landon, and I decided to go. While I was bent over picking up my gear, Sgt. Mac got up and said, "Oh, my God, here they come!"

I stood up to see what it was all about and there were literally thousands of enemy troops with their tanks and other mechanized equipment advancing toward our line in battle formation.

In view of the situation, it goes without saying that those plans to go scouting were cancelled. Through our field communications the artillery was informed of the enemy's attack. Out artillery immediately opened fire, as the guns were already zeroed in on the path the enemy was most likely to take. I don't know how to describe what we witnessed, as a spectacular event or tragic event. The enemy was caught directly by our artillery and we could see pieces of equipment, as well as human bodies flying all over the place. Yet, the enemy kept on coming. At one time the enemy got so close to our line of defense our artillery had to cease firing for fear that it may get us. We engaged the enemy and a relatively small number of men held our position for two or three hours or longer.

We ran out of ammunition for the mortars, so I sent the three ammo carriers for more. Contrary to all our instructions and training to never shoot your mortars at the distance of less than 150 yards, we were shooting them almost vertically. As a result, mortar shells were bursting 100 yards or less from our own position. That's how close the enemy was to us; but we were entrenched so well we had the advantage over them, just as they had the advantage over us at Normandy.

When the ammo carriers returned, they brought no ammunition. Instead, they brought orders from the headquarters for us to withdraw. We were glad to hear that for we knew it was just a matter of time before we would be crushed by the enemy. The man in charge of this detail was a Lt. Landon. He was a very capable leader and a brave man, although at times he had a mean streak, bordering on cruelty.

Upon receiving orders for withdrawal, he, in turn, issued his own: "Listen you men," he said, "all non-coms (non-commissioned officers) remain here while the enlisted men withdraw. You, the enlisted men, take position in such and such a place and return fire and try to keep the enemy pinned down until we withdraw." We did just that, and it worked fine. We withdrew to our main line of defense and within ten minutes the enemy was upon us. For six days and nights we were under constant enemy attack, which we repulsed and we held our ground. The only time we could come out of our foxholes, even for our necessities, was when our planes came to attack the enemy. We called these men "Glamour Boys," not in a derogatory way, but affectionately, for we, the "doughboys," loved them, truly.

During one of these breaks while our "glamour boys" were above us and silenced the enemy guns I ran, like other G.I. s to draw my rations and mail from home, if any, and I hit the jackpot; there was a bundle for me consisting of forty-two letters from my wife, the first letters I received from her since I had left the United States for overseas duty. And, again, thanks to the cover from our "glamour boys," I was able to sort the mail, put it in order according to the days, and read the letters. That's when I found out that I was a father of a son! Up to this point, as I've said, I hoped to stay alive at least until I knew whether I had a son or a daughter. Now that I knew I was a father of a son I didn't want to be killed until I met him.

On the 6th day, towards the latter part of the afternoon, a patrol from our side came to conduct a reconnaissance. Soon after, the same patrol was returning.

It stopped by us and the leader of the patrol said: "Listen youse [sic] guys, tomorrow morning there is going to be a lot of noise here. But relax, and don't worry because most of the noise is going to be ours." With that the patrol departed. We anxiously awaited the next morning. At daybreak our artillery opened up a terrific barrage, and simultaneously an American mechanized unit was advancing. It was an incredibly magnificent spectacle, watching the tanks move into position for an attack that was about to take place. They, the tanks and antitank weapons, moved forward slowly and very quietly. This unit was the very famous Second Mechanized American Division, better known as "Hell on Wheels." Right after the artillery ceased firing, the mechanized unit attacked and broke through the enemy lines in a very short time.

21
Experience in Belgium

After the spectacular breakthrough, we chased the enemy all the way to Belgium. We marched on foot for three days and part of the nights. We met very strong resistance, but after some skirmishes we broke their resistance and swiftly continued the chase.

While we were marching, the company commander fell out of rank and waited until I caught up with him. He started to walk alongside me and engaged me in conversation.

"Sergeant," he said, "I heard that congratulations are in order." "What about, sir?"

"I was told you were the father of a son."

"Oh, yes, captain. That's right. In one of her letters my wife told me that we have a son."

He extended his congratulations and asked me, "What are you going to name him?"

"Alfred. Alfred Joseph."

"Oh, no! You're not going to name your son Alfred, are you?"

"Why nor, what is wrong with that name, sir?"

"Why don't you name him Michael or Mike?"

"I like these names that you suggested, Captain, but our people never will call him those. He would be either Michel or Mich, and I don't like those names. Besides, his grandmother speaks only Basque and we like to give him a name that she can pronounce. He will be called either Al or Fred, and his grandmother will be able to pronounce either name without difficulty."

"You are right, sergeant. I was just kidding. I do wish to extend my congratulations to you, and I wish the best of luck to you, to your wife, and your son."

"Thank you very much, captain." With that he left me and accelerated his steps to again take the lead of the column.

This man, our company commander who was known amongst us as "Captain Dusty," was the man who busted me from staff sergeant to private because of the remark I made at chow: "Is that for everybody or just for the 'old men'?" We became good friends.

In the last day of our trek advancing toward Belgium we were picked up by the Army trucks, and late at night we pulled off the road and stopped for the rest of the night. Some men stayed in the trucks, others got off the trucks and looked for a dry spot to get some rest, but there weren't any dry spots to be found. Two of those that got off the truck were my best buddies, Sergeants Trent and Papadakos. The three of us went looking for some straw, a barn, or something dry. After walking a quarter of a mile or so, we heard people talking. We stopped and listened to see if we could determine what language they were speaking. We realized that we were at the very edge of a town or village, and it dawned on us that the town might be full of Germans. We listened carefully and concluded that they were speaking French.

I told my buddies, "They are speaking French."

"You sure?"

"Yes, I am sure."

"Should we go to the village?"

After a brief discussion, sort of a summit conference, we decided to go into the village. We moved cautiously and came across a street. I should have said that because of the blackout it was difficult to distinguish anything, but after we got to the street we knew for sure that we were in a town because of the nearness of the sound of the voices. We knew that we were surrounded by people, but couldn't see them due to the blackout. We moved nervously down the street with our weapons at the "port arms" position; ready to use them. Pretty soon somebody beamed a flashlight on us, then another, and yet another. They realized that we were not Germans. Someone said "L'Anglise!" and passed the word "L'Anglise, l'Anglise." I told my buddies that these people think we are English.

They kept on yelling the "l'Anglise," until I said: "No. No. l'Americain." "Oh, l'Americain!" Some of them with flashlights came closer to us and shook hands with us. We were led to a house by a well-wishing couple and many of their friends. It was a terrific reception. In their house they drew the curtains and turned the lights on. They served us wine, cognac, bread, ham and all kinds of meats, things that they had been saving or hiding from the Germans. They shared everything they had with us. Someone participating in the party brought a young man with an accordion, and he played some of their national music. A few couples danced. It was a real party. Towards the wee hours of the morning the lady of the house admonished everybody to be quiet, by placing her right index finger on her lips and exclaiming "Shhh." Everyone became quiet; the music stopped. We could hear a baby crying in an adjoining room. The lady, the mother of the child, went to the adjoining room and returned with the crying child in her arms. I approached her, extending my arms, silently asking if I could hold the child. She gave the baby to me, and I held it. I don't know whether it was a boy or a girl; all I know is that it was a good feeling to hold it. The baby was about the age of Alfred. While I held it in my arms, I thought of him.

Soon after that the party broke up. I was worried, wondering whether our outfit had moved on while we were gone. No need to worry; it was just where we left it.

At daylight we were told to set up camp in the area where we stopped the night before. We were to draw our pup tents from the trucks that brought them to us, and everybody scattered, scouting all over the area looking for necessary things like water. The three of us, Trent, Papadakos and I went on "scouting" through the town. People were all over the town, most of them in front of their homes waving and greeting us. As we were walking along the streets of this little town, we came across a house on the outskirts where a family was standing in front of it, waving at us.

The man of the house came to meet us in the middle of the street and said: "Bon jour Monsieur."

My friends asked "What did he say?"

I said, "He said 'good day, gentlemen'." I said: «Bon jour, monsieur. «Comment ca va?»

"Tres bien!" and believing that I spoke French he kept on speaking to us in French, not realizing that he had lost me after the last phrase. Nevertheless, we were somehow able to communicate. He motioned us to follow him. We followed him to his home, shook hands with every member of the family, and tried to talk with them.

The main thing that we were looking for was water, so I asked him, in what I thought to be French, "Je Vodrei L'eau." I didn't know how to say "we." That was supposed to mean: I want some water. Whether it does or not I don't know; but he must have understood part of the sentence because he provided water, soap and towels for us.

They fed us some homemade goodies and coffee. We protested, but they insisted we have breakfast with them. After breakfast the lady of the house wanted to show us something. She made us understand, by sign language and motions, that she wanted us to follow her. We did! All of us; the three G.I.s, and her family. She led us to a building in the enclosed yard in back of the house. She led us into the barn and turned the light on. There it was, the biggest pig I had ever seen in my life! The lady pointed her finger at it and explained to us all about it, but we did not understand anything she said except the word "Hitler." The big pig was named "Hitler," and she wanted us to know it.

We stayed in this town for several days which, incidentally, was not in France. It was in Belgium and the name of it was Lesdain. French is one of the three official languages spoken in Belgium.

It was in this town on September 2nd, 1944, that I received a telegram from home notifying me of the birth of our son. It was dated July 6, 1944. As I have said before, by that time I knew that he was born.

During our stay in this little village we made many friends and daily visited, and sometimes dined, with different families. They fed us very well. We felt guilty taking all the food from them (chickens, ducks, rabbits or whatever they had), as we realized the shortage of food they had gone through during the occupation by the Germans. We tried to reciprocate by taking our rations to them as much as we could, but to no avail. The next time we dined with them, our "reciprocity" was prepared and given back to us. Perhaps they felt that they owed us something and wanted to share what little they had with us. From what I could observe, they were very appreciative and generous. We fell in love with them, and I am sure that the feeling was mutual.

On the eve of our departure from this town, which was widely heralded throughout the village, we visited our friends, the family who owned "Hitler the pig." The family consisted of father, mother, three daughters and a son. They invited us (when I say us, I mean the three of us; Trent, Papadakos and I) to attend Mass on the day of our departure, and have breakfast with the family. We accepted the invitation, and on the following morning we went to their house and we all went to the church. When it was time for Communion, the family stood up and proceeded to the altar. I, as a Catholic, followed them, and my two friends followed me; the three of us, like the "Three Musketeers." I don't know of what religion my friends were affiliated, but in circumstances such as these, everybody wanted to be close to Jesus, including me. So, disregarding the religious affiliations, we tried to be close to him the best way we knew how, and my friends received their Communion.

From the church we went to our friends' home for breakfast, and at about noon we had to leave to get ready for our departure.

Around 5:00 p.m. the trucks came to pick us up. To me it seemed as though the whole town was present to see us leave. During the few days that we were in this village we developed a very real affection for each other. Many of them cried. They were sad. They knew that we were heading to the front lines, and there was always the possibility that many of their new American friends would not return. The departure from Lesdain was a sad and memorable day for its people, as well as for us.

22
Ambush in Pussey

In view of the fact that the Allies were already in Belgium, the Germans, realizing that they were going to be trapped, retreated as fast as they could after the Allied invasion of the Marseille sector. That is why our division was sent from Belgium to Pussey, which is in the northeastern part of France, to set up position to stop the German retreat. In this town of Pussey as we were moving along, one of our Piper Cub planes spotted a large column of the enemy moving north. The column consisted of all kinds of enemy troops and equipment, some mechanized units, soldiers riding bicycles, motorcycles, and other vehicles. We were not too far from this column when the piper Cub spotted it, so hurriedly we moved to the main highway, where this column was moving and set up an ambush.

The ambush consisted of placing a few tanks in front as a roadblock to stop them, and the rest of the troops deployed parallel with the highway on both sides. The idea was that as soon as our tanks opened up on the enemy's leading unit, and stopped the head of the column, the rest of us would shoot and destroy the enemy. The tanks were positioned and the rest of us were deployed along the highway to wait. Along about midnight we could hear the enemy approaching. We were as quiet as possible, but the number of the enemy troops was so great that there was no way that they could get by without being detected. About midnight the enemy was in the "pocket" of the ambush. The moment the tanks opened up we knew for sure that the enemy was trapped. As the tanks opened fire the columns stopped, and our orders were to shoot toward the enemy. After we opened fire the enemy got panicky, and from the yells, screams and crying it was obvious where the enemy was. From both sides we shot at them, and many of them, the smartest ones, the ones that were not so panicky, hit the ground and stayed there. Others, who were more frightened tried to break through our lines and were either killed, or wounded. Few, though, were captured. Our fire against them was intense and accurate. Everything that we had, rifles, machine guns (both 30 and 50 caliber machine guns) and mortars were aimed at them, with no return fire from the enemy. After things quieted down a little, there were many Germans who wanted to surrender, but it was difficult for them to do so. If they tried to get through our lines at night, they knew they were going to be shot. The G.I.s could not take a chance in capturing them either for we never knew if they would be armed with hand grenades, or what their intentions might be. However, in our sector where our mortar section was, there were two Germans that wanted to surrender—we could tell there were at least two from the different sounds of the soldiers. They were yelling and talking to us in German, usually they said, "Americain," or "Camarade." They sounded pitiful. I knew that they wanted to surrender, but no one answered them. Soon one of the two rushed through the line and someone from the platoon adjoining ours yelled, "Halt!" The German kept coming. Instantly, after the command to "halt," the men opened fire and killed him. We were on a sunken road with our mortars, and we could hear the wounded or dead German rolling in this meadow over to the sunken road. Everything was quiet, very quiet. His companion, realizing what had happened, started yelling, undoubtedly telling us he wanted to surrender and that he was "clean," but we did not understand, and soon he was crying, really crying aloud. Everyone was tense wondering what was going to be next. In this silence, the German evidently crawled on his belly towards the sunken road, lowered himself down, and rushed towards us where we were right in front of a big barn. At the door of the barn, the German came directly into my arms. I grabbed him and wrestled him down. Two or three other men came to help. We were all excited. I told the men, "Don't shoot him, don't shoot him, he's done!" They did not intend to shoot him. They did not even touch him, for they knew I had the guy subdued. I searched him. He didn't have anything—no grenades, no pistol, no weapons of any kind. After a minute or two he started crying more than before, and I think they were tears of joy, realizing he had not been shot by anybody in our lines after he surrendered. I stood up, pulled him up with me, and took him to a corner inside the barn where the guys turned flashlights on him to see what he looked like. Soon he built up enough confidence to ask for a cigarette. We understood that by sign language. Someone gave him a cigarette, and a minute or two later he asked for "chocolate." Someone gave him a candy bat that he had in his pack as a reserve ration, and the German was smoking, eating candy and crying at the same time—so pitiful in his hysterical crying.

There was no sleep that night, like many other nights. In the morning we noticed several officers instructing our leaders as we were moving toward the highway, designating each platoon to different details. The details consisted of clearing the highway of debris and the dead enemy. As we were moving toward the highway, the area was full of dead and wounded Germans, and hundreds of prisoners. When the attack started, those who hit the ground and stayed there until daylight were lucky, and there was no problem taking them as prisoner. You didn't have to go after them. They had already surrendered. Our job was to clean up the highway. The dead and wounded Germans were found on either side of the highway for about 250 yards. There were hundreds of dead Germans, maybe thousands. We commenced cleanup operations. There were several platoons, maybe a full company, removing the dead and piling them up in what seemed to me little plots of gardens or orchards. Most of the dead were carried by four soldiers to each dead man. They would swing, "One, two, three" and throw the body over a three or four foot stone wall that served as a fence. In some other vacant areas, there were American and German medics administering first-aid to the wounded Germans. As for equipment, there were hundreds, possibly thousands, of bicycles, motorcycles, innumerable automobiles, American jeeps, personnel carriers, some trucks, bigger equipment such as tanks, and that kind of equipment. Most of the day was spent in clearing the debris. Trucks, tanks and heavier equipment were all removed by our bulldozers.

23
Entertainment on the Front Line

After accomplishing our mission in Pussey, we moved east. During one of these occasions, as we were advancing, our regiment was designated to be the reserve unit. We bivouacked in a particular place and were notified that there was going to be some entertainment (for those of us who were in the reserve) that afternoon. The main protagonists of the show" were to be Bing Crosby and Diana Shore. It surprised me that these people would come that close to the front line, actually exposed to enemy artillery.

Only a few G.I.s remained in the bivouac. Everyone went to see and hear the celebrities. They were only three or four blocks from where I was. I remember one of the songs they sang in duet, "San Antonio Rose." That kind of thing did nothing to build my morale. Instead of going to see and hear them, I stayed in camp and wrote a letter to my wife. In the evening, two or three hours after the show, we were supposed to have some religious services in the same place where the show was held to be conducted by a Catholic priest. Everybody went to these services, including me, but the priest did not make it due to bad weather, rain, and muddy roads. After waiting for the priest for a long time, and realizing that he wasn't going to show up, an officer, a captain, stood up, walked to the podium or make-shift altar, called for our attention, and explained why the priest couldn't come.

"But," the captain said, "since we have gathered here for this purpose let us have some sort of services of our own." To me this man was a true leader. I do not know what religion he belonged to, and it did not matter. He quoted a passage or two from the Bible, then offered a prayer. Again, he quoted from the Bible and asked those present to say, "Jesus Christ taught us, Our Father, etc." For me this man did more to build the morale of a G.I. than all of those "celebrities" from

Hollywood. He was a leader. I often think of him, even now. What became of him? Did he have a wife and maybe a child or two? He was a strong, religious man, and very brave man. Did he come home to them? To his loved ones? I hope so!

The following morning we continued our advance. We met a very tough resistance in a certain area. It was a forest and the enemy was positioned at the very edge of it, waiting for us. There was a cleared area of three or four hundred yards before we could get to them. We attacked, but from their advantageous position out attack was repulsed, with the Germans inflicting many casualties on us. We tried again, but with the same results. Finally, our company commander (my friend Captain Dusty), re-fused to attack again unless we received some artillery support, claiming that it was suicide to attack the enemy under those cir-cumstances. He won, and soon after, before our third charge, our artillery laid a fantastic barrage against them, and for the first and only time during my career in the Army, we attacked the enemy with fixed bayonets under a smoke screen. Really spec-tacular, even though I do say so myself.

When we reached the enemy's line of defense, they were gone. In our particular sector (that is our section's sector), there was only one German. I thought that he was dead for he was in his foxhole with his face resting on the ground and his left arm stretched forward, displaying his wristwatch. The man next to me carrying a B.A.R. (Browning Automatic Rifle), reached for his wrist.

The German instinctively pulled his arm back and the man with the B.A.R. asked the platoon sergeant, who was next to him on the right, "Sarge, this guy is alive. What should I do?"

The sergeant, without hesitation, replied, "Shoot the bas-tard!"

The man with the B.A.R. shot him! It was a first degree murder! There was no reason for it. Both of these men showed their sadistic inclinations. This German wanted to surrender, and he thought he had his opportunity to do so; but we shot him. The man who shot him no doubt felt it was justified. First, because the sergeant told him to shoot him, and second, "This is war!" In my opinion both of these men should have been court marshalled, and perhaps executed.

Among us there were all kinds of men. The great majority of our men were strong, solid, compassionate men, who fought well. There were among us some who, in spite of the difficult circumstances, had a terrific sense of humor. There were a few like the ones I described above, sadists and others who could be classified as vultures, whose main objective seemed to be to search through bodies of friends and foes alike for valuables, and, if they find anything valuable, remove it. A classic example: Soon after the killing I have just described, two men came upon his body and proceeded to search it. One of the men removed the wrist-watch and the wedding ring from the body. The other grabbed the body by the collar and jerked it back exposing the dead German's face. It was so grotesque, with distorted features and blood. The G.I. searched it and found nothing but a few letters and some pictures, no doubt of his wife and children. What a price to pay for a man who wanted to surrender!

24
Vosges Mountains Attack

In our advance, we entered another forest, but didn't get in too far because of the enemy's strong resistance. Later we were told that out division commander had made a mistake in engaging with the enemy in the forest. We were supposed to bypass it and trap the enemy there, but the Germans outsmarted us. The battle raged for days. It was a very dangerous place to be. Sometimes I counted twenty and more enemy mortar shells being fired. I counted them. All these rounds were up in the air at the same time and then I counted them again as they started to hit the ground and explode, sweating and grinding my teeth until the last one exploded, expecting any one of them to score a direct hit. This was continuous, every day and night.

One evening we got orders to be ready to attack the enemy the following morning. We were ready, and at daybreak we moved to assault. As we were moving forward, the chaplain was there with the Holy Host in his hands to give Communion to us. Most of the men took it, while moving into battle positions. A spectacular artillery fire followed. We moved on and the artillery kept on pounding the enemy just a few yards ahead of us. The accuracy of its fire was incredible. As we were advancing, our artillery also kept increasing the range and laid a devastating fire just a few yards ahead of us. The enemy, we learned later, consisted exclusively of German SS troops. They were yelling, screaming, crying, and surrendering by the hundreds, literally.

After dislodging them from the forest, we moved forward

towards the Vosges Mountains in Alsace-Lorraine. Incidentally, the 79th Division shoulder patch (the Lorraine Cross) which consisted of a vertical bar and two horizontal bars, shorter above and longer below, is almost like the symbol for T.B. (tuberculosis).

We were told that we were to attack and take possession of a certain area of high ground in the Vosges Mountains, repulse the enemy's counter attacks, hold our position for at least forty-eight hours, and then we were going to be relieved and sent to a rest area. We did just that. In passing I wish to say that the Germans we captured in these woods removed all insignias or anything that could identify them as SS Troops, and they all seemed to claim to be Polish, Czechoslovakian, or anything but Germans, "forced" to fight for Germany.

After reaching our objective, we dug in as usual. I left the mortar section four or five hundred yards behind and went ahead with the riflemen to dig my own foxhole. We observed some enemy activity in front of us. I was ordered to investigate, and should I spot an enemy patrol in reconnaissance, destroy it with mortars. In order to do so I carried one end of the wire to connect to the field phone in case I needed it to issue the fire order. I did not hear anything, and it was impossible to see anything or anybody, as it was dark. When I reached the end of the cable of the field phone, I signaled the main line of the results of my exploration and I was ordered to return. I was glad when I was given that order. It had been a suicidal mission. During the night I went to join the men of my section.

Early in the morning the enemy attacked. Between our company and the company to our right was a gap of several hundred yards. To close the gap an outpost was set up consisting of a fifty caliber machine gun (with its corresponding crew), and a few riflemen which the enemy over ran, killing everyone who was manning it. The enemy poured through this gap and surrounded us.

As this happened so suddenly, I didn't have a chance to get to my foxhole with the riflemen, so when the shooting began I jumped into the closest slit trench, which belonged to a man who was happy to share it with me. His name was Alex (I don't know his surname). He was American of Jewish descent and spoke German, in addition to English, of course. Suddenly, two or three tanks came out of the woods. They were ours. They opened fire and the missiles they fired towards the enemy went whizzing over our heads and quickly stopped the enemy's fire. Some of the Germans withdrew toward their line. We spotted one of them running fast and zigzagging towards his line. Everybody was shooting at him, but not getting him.

The men of the weapons platoon carried small guns, either forty-five caliber pistols or carbines. That was because the weapons such as machine guns, mortars (and the ammunition for them that had to be carried), was so heavy that the men were issued lighter weapons. Being the section leader I did not have to carry any particular weapon. I could carry a forty-five caliber pistol, a carbine or an M-1 rifle which I usually chose to do.

At this particular time and place I was the only man carrying an M-1 rifle. Everyone began to shoot at him, but he was well beyond the small weapons range, except for me, yet he made it to his lines safely. When I was herding sheep in the Owyhees I always carried a rifle with which I could hit anything, jack rabbits, coyotes, crows, magpies, anything. Yet I couldn't hit this German, even though he was within the range of my M-1! I was relieved when I saw him make it to the safety of his lines. I could have gotten this man with my rifle, but my conscience, war or peace, prevented me from shooting him, as it would have been shooting a man in the back. I aimed at him and had him in my rifle's peep sight. I jerked my weapon deliberately to miss him. Perhaps those G.I.s around me were thinking, 'What kind of soldier is this man? But, no, I don't think so, because these men, the G.I.s I speak of, were good, solid, hard fighting men, fighting for a cause, but men with compassion; one of the greatest virtues bestowed on mankind by the Supreme Being. They knew what I was doing and why, but instead of criticizing me, they just smiled!

When things quieted down I asked Alex to ask the enemy to surrender, since he could speak German. He did, and to our surprise two of them came out of their hiding with their hands clasped behind their helmets. I felt it was my obligation as the section leader to search them. I asked the men to cover me and I proceeded to search the Germans. They were clean (no concealed weapons). Obviously the other Germans surrounding us were observing and realizing that they were safe. Judging from the treatment the two first prisoners received from us, more Germans decided to surrender. A batch of 10 to 15 men surrendered. A couple of other men came to help me search them and we found them unarmed. We did find American made cigarettes on them which had been taken from our American dead or prisoners.

I think that I had mentioned before that we were to hold the enemy in this spot for forty-eight hours before our replacements would arrive and we could go to a rest area. The forty-eight hours was prolonged to seventy-two. We held the enemy for that long before our relief finally arrived.

25
Rest After 137 Days of Combat

We were anxiously awaiting our relief to come and take over our positions. Finally, they arrived towards evening. It was almost dark when someone brought a staff sergeant, my counterpart of the mortar section, of the unit that was to relieve us. We shook hands and I showed him the location of our foxholes which they were about to take over. He counted eight of them.

"Where are the test of the holes?" he asked me. I replied that there weren't any more. We were only eight men left from twenty, so we only needed eight foxholes; some of his men would have to dig their own holes. He was not too happy about that. I went with him to greet his men. They were all neat guys. They had never been in combat yet. They would receive their "baptism of fire" here.

As our men were vacating the foxholes, and the reliefs moving into them, the enemy opened fire on us. We scrambled for cover.

I heard one man, a newcomer, say: "It is coming from that direction. Let's get them."

"O.K.," replied another man "let's go." The first man thought he knew where the machine gun or "burp gun" that was firing on us was located because he could see (as all of us could) from the direction of the tracer bullets. They stood up and staffed out towards where they thought the shooting was coming from. I don't know what the outcome was of their investigation. We received orders to form a column and move out with the rest of our unit. I have an idea that they were ordered to stop by an officer or, realizing the futility of trying to take the "nest" over single-handed, were discouraged, but that I do not know.

As we were marching towards our rest area, other units merged with us forming a very long single file of tired G.I.s.

We marched all night through the wet, muddy paths and trails, always subject to the enemy's sporadic artillery barrages. I felt sorry for those men who relieved us and thought about them all during the night while marching.

After marching all night, we arrived at out test area at daybreak. It was a small village at the foot of the Vosges Mountains. When we arrived our replacements were there. I remember three young men from Boston, Massachusetts. All three of them graduates from the University of Massachusetts. As "living quarters" for our rest period we were assigned a fairly good-sized barn with a hayloft. The three men that I have mentioned were the only three of the nine our section received. These three stand out in my mind because of a couple of incidents. Two of the men's names were Bill. The third was Frank. I do not remember their surnames.

After a month of being involved in some tough battles, Frank came to me in a lull period, and told me: "Sarge," he said, "I want to tell you something."

"Like what?" I asked.

"When I first met you in front of that barn, our resting quarters, you scared me. I was afraid of you. There you were with a pitch black beard, bloodshot eyes, a gun slung on your back, the ugliest trench knife strapped to your leg and you were removing mud from your clothes with a bayonet. I thought I was looking at the meanest man I had ever seen in my life. But I want to tell you, that after getting to know you better, I think you are one of the best men I have ever known. I mean that, Sarge," he said and left. What a nice compliment, I thought.

I think that his feelings towards me were perhaps personal. He was a rather small man and sometimes in prolonged marches it was very difficult for him to carry, the ammunition (which ammo bag contained six 60mm mortar shells). On those occasions I helped him carry them. I picked up his bag and carried it myself, instead of yelling at him like many of the movies or T.V. programs depict, sergeants screaming at their subordinates. However, the main reason I remember these three is the following incident I would like to describe.

While we were in a bivouac, the three friends came to me and announced that they were going "over the hill" (A.W.O.L.) (absent without leave). They came to the conclusion that they would never make it fighting the Germans—so they decided that the only way to survive was to desert the Army.

"Sarge," the spokesman for them said, "we are deserting."

"Really?" I said. "If you are caught I am sure that you are aware of the serious consequences."

"Yes, we are. We hate to do this, but we feel that it is the only way to save our skins. The problem is," he continued, "that we want to go to Luxembourg, but we don't know which way it is. Could you tell us?"

I was amazed that these three college graduates were asking me for directions to Luxembourg, from the area where we were in France! I told them that I didn't exactly know where Luxembourg was, but I could give them the general direction, which I did.

The following day we assembled to move forward. At the roll call three men were missing. The officer in command wanted to know where they were. Since they were members of my section he asked me, "Where are those men?"

"I don't know, sir. Maybe they are asleep in the foxholes. Let me check, sir." I went to check their foxholes knowing that they were not there. They did go A.W.O.L.

26
Return to the Front Line

The rest period that came after 137 consecutive days at the front lasted eighteen days. The first few days of the rest were a nightmare. Some of us chose to settle in the hayloft of a barn. It was cozy, lots of dry hay for a mattress, and pretty comfortable. But we all had very bad dreams. It seemed as though the enemy was chasing and shooting at us all the time. Men woke up screaming in the middle of the night. It was also dangerous in the loft, because in our dreams someone might start walking and fall from the loft which was at least twelve feet from the floor of the barn.

The family who owned the barn consisted of a father, mother and three daughters, age 21, 19 and 17.

The town was small, perhaps 200 people or less and although it was less than 22 kilometers from the sizeable town of Lunaville the girls had never been in it. While resting in this village we had hot meals and a dry place to sleep.

One day at chow time we formed a line as usual and our company commander, Capt. Dusty, called for our attention. "Let me have your attention, please," he said. "I know that most of you men are wondering why we did not hear from Sgt. Papadakus. I just received word from regimental headquarters that he passed away in a hospital as the result of injuries he suffered in such and such a battle. The reason for his silence was that he couldn't write. Let us bow our heads and offer him a 30-second silent prayer."

I think that every company in the army had a "character." Ours was Sgt. Papadakus. He was a rather small, wiry man. A good, loyal American soldier of Greek descent with an unsurpassed sense of humor. There are many, too many humorous incidents about him to relate here. I just want to describe only one. We were in a very hot spot, and when I say hot, I don't mean because of atmospheric conditions, but of the shellacking we were getting from the enemy. He yelled at me: "Kashpar! Kashpar!"

I stuck my head out of the foxhole and could see a foot sticking out of his foxhole. Even in situations like that he had the ability to make a joke and induce laughter in his friends. What he was trying by sticking his foot out of the foxhole was that he was wishing that he would be hit in the foot and sent back. I did laugh at the joke. However, he was hit later on, but not in his foot, in his lung. I saw a medic carrying him on his (medic's) shoulders. I ran up to him. But Papadakus was unconscious and couldn't talk to me. I followed him for a while. He was emitting a mixture of slobber and blood from his mouth. I talked to him but he never answered me. He was critically wounded, and, as a result, he died in the hospital.

The day of our departure from this place was the Armistice Day, 1944. We packed all our equipment to go into battle, but first we had to take part in commemoration of the Armistice in Lunaville. After the parade we were packed in the trucks again and were taken to the front and renewed our pursuit of the enemy. A few days after this event I developed a very bad toothache that got to the point that I couldn't stand it. One day I asked our company commander for permission to go see a dentist and relieve my problem. He granted my request and arranged for me to go to the nearest hospital and have the tooth extracted. The following day, while we were waiting on top of a hill contemplating an attack on the town named Baccarat, the company commander revoked my request to go see a dentist. Instead, I was instructed to be ready for the attack with bayonets on the town of Baccarat in the morning. So many times we were to attack with bayonets, yet we never met the enemy with bayonets, they always ran before we got to them. Because of that the G.I.s spread rumors that the Germans used their bayonets as can openers to open their ration cans, and never sharpened them. The G.I.'s sense of humor was incredibly beautiful.

We launched the attack at daybreak but met no resistance, as the enemy, contemplating our attack, had left their positions during the night.

At midday I got permission from the company commander to go take care of my tooth. I got a tide in a jeep to go to the dentist. That afternoon he extracted my tooth. He had a lot of trouble in doing so, and decided to keep me overnight and the following day. On the third day, which was Thanksgiving, he discharged me. I was told that there was a truck leaving for our battalion H.Q. (headquarters) and that I could ride in it. The truck was loaded to the brim. There was only one other passenger besides me and we accommodated ourselves by the tailgate of the truck.

We stopped at some outfit's headquarters for lunch and were told that their outfit was having turkey for dinner, so we got regular rations for lunch. We moved on toward our destination after lunch, and towards the latter part of the afternoon reached a village. As we were crossing it, I recognized a lot of my buddies foaming around. I came to the conclusion that my outfit, the Company C, must be here. I yelled at the truck driver to stop, but he couldn't hear me. I picked up my gear and jumped from the truck while it was in motion.

I was right. My company was here. I met some of my buddies and someone asked me: "Did you have anything to eat for supper?"

"No," I said.

"That is too bad," he said. "I'll get you something. We had turkey for lunch. I'll get you some rations."

So I missed the Thanksgiving turkey dinner completely. When the truck got into headquarters and I wasn't there, I was reported as A.W.O.L.

We kept on moving toward Germany at a very fast pace. We usually took possession and set up a defense by digging in at the highest point.

In one of the towns, or outskirts of it, while we were digging in, who should come to see me but my three "student friends" who had gone A.W.O.L.!

"Hi, Sarge."

"Hello Sarge."

"We are back, Sarge."

The conversation went pretty much like that. I asked them what happened and why they had come back. Their story was that their conscience bothered them about leaving us behind fighting the enemy, while they went seeking safety for themselves. They decided to return and take their chances with the rest of us.

Then they asked me "What are they going to do to us?"

"Nothing." I said. "I am sure that there will be no reprisals. In fact, everybody will be glad to see that you are back. The only punishment you might suffer will be inflicted by the enemy, and we are all subject to that."

With that we went looking for some equipment for them, guns, packs, ammo, etc. The following day we moved on swiftly towards Germany, taking many cities, among them Kurtzenhousen, Biestwiller, Lauterburg, and others. Some of the men seemed to doubt my student friends' story. Some thought that they came back because the chances of them making it were almost nonexistent. I chose to believe their story because I found them to be honest and decent young men.

In our advance we encountered many tough enemy strongholds, and as the result of their stubborn resistance we fought many hard battles. One of them was on a hill which was a part of the defense network of the city of Kurtzenhausen. The battle for that hill began at daybreak, and we took possession of it in the latter part of the afternoon. Under the heavy fire of our artillery protection we advanced slowly. While moving upward on our bellies we went by many of our men that were dead or wounded. One of the dead I recognized as the one who removed the wristwatch and the wedding ring from the German unnecessarily killed. I thought that perhaps this was God's punishment. Finally, we broke their resistance and reached their line. From then on the dead and wounded were the enemy.

The shooting ceased and while we were walking through the destroyed enemy line, two Germans came out of nowhere and surrendered to our section. I searched them and found them clean of any weapons. One, if not both of them, spoke English, although with a very pronounced German accent. He told me something about some wounded Germans. He was very concerned about them. He wanted to show me where they were because they, the wounded, needed some help. I told him to lead me to them. I suggested that the section move on and I would catch up with them. I asked them to take care of the second prisoner. I followed the prisoner, whom I talked to. What he showed me was horrible. He took me to a group of dead Germans, five in all, which was a mortar squad. It was completely destroyed, undoubtedly by our mortars. Just a little further on was another squad of Germans. Out of this group of five, one was dead and four were badly wounded. This was the result of our mortar's accuracy and efficiency again. One of the wounded spoke some English. He asked for help. There was nothing I could do for them. I tried to make the one I spoke to more comfortable by propping his head up, as it was on a downgrade, and told him that American medics will take care of them soon and then I took my prisoner and left. We stopped not far from them for the night until daylight for the final assault on Kurtzenhousen. It rained all night and it was very cold. It was miserable. We were wet, cold, hungry, tired and, of course, afraid, anticipating what would take place the next day. The wounded sporadically started yelling, screaming, and crying in their pain.

In one of those periods of their screaming our lieutenant came out of the shelter found for him and his staff, cussing and said: "I am going to put an end to them," and I heard him cock his pistol. I was very close to the shelter.

I told the lieutenant: "Sir, you don't need to do that. Our medics will pick them up soon."

"How do you know?" he replied.

"Because they (the medics) told me so." This was not true. I didn't talk to the medics, but it was our policy.

He let out another burst of obscenities and said: "They better because if they don't, I will finish these b . . . ."

Well, the lieutenant, didn't need to finish them. The wounded men did not utter another sound during the rest of the night. This was the lieutenant I mentioned in one of the previous chapter who was a brave soldier and good leader, but mean, sometimes bordering on cruelty.

The following morning we began the advance towards our next objective, which was the City of Kurtzenhousen. As we started our march I decided to go see the wounded enemy. I told the men of my section that I would catch up with them soon. Out of the four remaining alive the evening before, three were dead. The only one alive was the one I talked to. That was the reason that after the lieutenant's outburst the wounded did not cry out. I talked to this man again. He was badly mutilated. He asked me for something to drink.

I pulled my water canteen and started to give him some water.

"No, No," he said. "Something hot."

I did not have anything hot to give to him. We didn't even have any Nescafe, nothing hot even before we started our march. I told him so. Again, I told him that the American medics will pick him up.

He said: "You told me that yesterday!"

I knew that he did not believe me, but it was our policy to pick up our own wounded first and later, if possible, the wounded enemy.

27
Advance to the Siegfried Line

Early the following morning, we moved on to our next objective, the city of Kurtzenhousen in Alsace-Lorraine. After a tough battle, we took possession of it and settled in for the night. We set up our outposts on the outskirts of the town to protect us from the enemy's possible counterattacks. We set up our schedule to man the outposts, and found a place in town to spend the night. It was a place, sort of a catacomb, almost like a cave, but it was manmade. Everybody was warming their coffee or rations and the place was full of smoke with no outlets for its dissipation. Since it was approaching Christmas, the men tried to get in the mood for the season, so in this smoke-filled cavern they started to sing Christmas carols. There were these men, fighting men, many of them will be killed in a few hours, thinking of their homes, their families, wives and children. Their singing surely brought memories to me, particularly when they sang "Silent Night," which is my favorite carol. When they came to the line "Mother and Child," my mind flew 10,000 kilometers to Jordan Valley, Oregon, U.S.A. where my wife and son were "mother and child"! and wondered: "Will I ever see them and hold them in my arms?" I wanted to join these men in singing carols, but I couldn't because I did not know any songs in English.

The following morning we moved on again. This time our objective was the town of Bistweiller. I am sure that I am not spelling it right, but phonetically it sounds right. The battle for Bistweiller was spectacular. As usual it started with the artillery barrage that included everything, mortars, short and long range artillery, as well as the incendiary shells which looked as if they were 4th of July fireworks. What made it more spectacular was the fact that when we broke through and entered the town with our fixed bayonets while the enemy was running, probably at the sight of our bayonets, there were hundreds of civilians watching our fight and witnessing and cheering us on with exclamations like "Vive l'Americains" "Vive la France" and "Bosh Caput," meaning that the Germans are gone. As we were going through the town, we searched some houses for snipers. I entered, alone, in one house and didn't see anybody on the ground floor. I decided to go to the basement, and, to my surprise there were two men there. They raised their hands and started talking very fast. I really scared them. I was not afraid of them because I could see that they were not armed and I had my M-1 pointed at them. One thing that I have always considered strange, even today, is that most of these people spoke some English. With the English language being as inconsistent as it is, I found it curious that it was so popular with foreigners. These two men who were in the basement also spoke some English. They told me that they were refugees from Holland. I believed them and planned to leave them there, but they insisted in coming out with me. They met other G.I.s and began to relax and smile. They felt pretty safe.

In one of the other houses we stopped at we found, instead of refugees, one room full from the floor to the ceiling with ladies' panties and brassieres. Someone was having a good business in bootlegging, which we ruined for him or her.

After spending the night in this town we proceeded to the town of Lautenburg, perhaps the last town of Alsace-Lorraine before reaching Germany. This fairly good-sized town was only six kilometers from the Rhine River.

After a tough battle, we dislodged the enemy and took possession of it in the late afternoon, spent the night in one of the empty houses, and moved on the following morning.

In less than ten minutes from the time that we vacated the house, and perhaps four or five blocks from it, we were subjected to a terrific artillery attack by the enemy. One of the shells hit directly on the house where some of us had spent the night and demolished it completely. We looked at each other, but never said a word, but we all knew what the other was thinking. If we had stayed there ten minutes longer all of us would have been gone.

There were several kinds of shells. I would like to describe the three shells that I was familiar with. One was a conventional shell that exploded at the touch of anything. Example: if this type of shell scores a direct hit, say in a house, it was scary but not very effective, because it explodes at the touch of the roof of the house. Therefore its fragments fly harmlessly rather than penetrate inside of the house. The "delayed action" shell did not detonate at the impact of it with the target, it would go through the roof and a few seconds later it would explode inside of the building and destroy everything. The air burst shells exploded automatically about 30 feet above the target and its fragments or shrapnel getting the men in their foxholes or slit trenches.

The city was at the edge of a forest. We got into this forest about noon on December 18, 1944. Around mid-afternoon we engaged the enemy. They opened fire on us and offered a tough resistance. Unknown to us until later, we came to the first stronghold of the Siegfried Line. We were told that because of the tough enemy resistance we needed additional forces to attack it and that we must wait until the following morning for the attack. The attack was set for 8:05 the following morning, December 19, 1944. The artillery duel was continuous from both sides. Towards the latter part of the evening, while my runner Louie and I were talking, a shell burst behind me. The explosion was very powerful. I saw stars in front of me just as if someone had punched me in the face. Louie, an American of Filipino descent, a tough, good and loyal soldier, lost his speech as the result of the concussion caused by that shell. I asked him to go to the medics, but he wouldn't because he didn't want to leave the rest of the men. When I said "my runner" I didn't mean to be immodest. In a mortar section a runner actually is a messenger for the section sergeant. He delivers messages, stretches the wire for the field telephones, etc. So when I said "my runner" I said it for easier understanding, rather than "our," as he was responsible only to the section leader.

Soon after this incident I decided to see our platoon sergeant, Charlie Bolera. After the attack and under constant enemy fire I crawled on my belly and found him. We talked about the tough situation, sitting on his slit trench. Charlie was very worried as to what might happen. I was too.

He said "Kashpar, we are not going to make it. I am the oldest member of this outfit." (Meaning that he was longest with the regiment, not oldest by age.) "Almost everybody that came with me is gone, so it is logical that I will be gone before too long."

He was trying to tell me something, so I asked him "Are you trying to tell me something, Sarge?"

"Yes, I am," he replied. "I think that in order to save our skins we should go A.W.O.L."

"Sergeant," I said, "you must be kidding!"

"No. The way you speak English (referring to my accent) all we have to do is buy a couple of berets and we can make it because with your language nobody will ever question us."

"Are you suggesting that you and I should be going A.W.O.L.?"

"Yes, I am, Kashpar. I have a premonition that we are not going to make it."

"Sarge. I have too much to lose. I have a wife and a son that I want to go back to. I am just as scared as anybody else, but I am going to take my chances. I took an oath to defend our country when I was granted the passport to come the U.S.A. Besides that, I want my wife and my son to be proud of me; particularly my son. I don't want him to grow up knowing that his father shirked his responsibilities and deserted him, his country, and his mother. Even if I don't make it back and am killed, I want him to be proud of his dad who died fulfilling his duty to his country. I think we have said enough about this, Sarge. I think I better go back to my men. Good night, Charley."

After a pause he said, "Good night, Kashpar. I will see you in the morning." and we parted company.

28
First Strong Point of the Siegfried Line

The following morning at the scheduled hour we launched our attack. As usual, it started with a frightful artillery fire. We, the infantry followed. We advanced on our bellies and just as soon as our artillery ceased firing, the enemy opened up on us. Our company's objective, which was only three or four hundred yards from the point where we started, was the very first strong point of the "Siegfried Line." It consisted of three well-fortified pill boxes. To reach and destroy them we had to cross an immense network of obstacles. First a deep, wide anti-tank trench, then a thick webbed-entanglement of barbed wire protected by riflemen, machine gun nests and mortars, then the pill boxes. We were told that the pill boxes were fortifications of cement walls, six to eight feet thick which were equipped with deadly 88 mm guns, mounted on a sophisticated hydraulic system. Our artillery scored a lot of direct hits, but we were unable to destroy them. The enemy's fire was fierce and inflicted a lot of casualties on us. While advancing very slowly I came across Sgt. Bolera (Charlie). The night before, when we departed company, he said to me: "I'll see you tomorrow." I saw him, but he did not see me for he was dead. His premonition was right. Moving on I also came across Sgt. Boyd, whom I knew well. He was wounded. He had a bullet in his shin and was screaming wildly because he was afraid that if the enemy repulsed our attack and he was made prisoner he was going to be killed by them because he had gobs and gobs of German marks (their money) taken away from the enemy prisoners.

He begged me to take the money, so in order to ease his mind I took it. I continued forward and again came across my friend Alex, the American Jew. He, too, was dead, and many others too numerous to describe.

In order to approach the enemy's fortifications we had to develop a path for the troops and the tanks on the anti-tank trench, but just as soon as our bulldozers attempted to build a ramp they were blown up by the enemy's 88mm from the pill boxes. Their fire on us (artillery, mortars and machine guns) was so intense that many of us jumped in the anti-tank trench seeking cover. It was a very serious mistake on our part because the enemy's guns were zeroed in on that trench, no doubt in anticipation that when they opened fire we would do just that, jump in the trench. The result was devastating.

From this trench our mortar fire was very effective against the enemy mortar and machine gun nests. We were able to eliminate them, and, in spite of the casualties we suffered, our bulldozers were able to build ramps for the use of the troops.

By crossing the trench through these ramps we were able to destroy the barbed wire entanglement with what I think were called "bangalore torpedoes." However, our tanks, although crossed the anti-tank trench, were unable to destroy the pill boxes. The only way that could be accomplished was by the demolition squads. The mission or duty of the demolition squads was to move just as close as possible to the pill boxes. By doing so the big guns were rendered ineffective against them at close range because of their limitations (they lose the flexibility of both deflection and range). That is, because of the small holes from which the guns were protruding, they could be lowered only so far and also deflect right or left only so far. Once our demolition squads got that close (right to the pill boxes), they lit the dynamite charges of the bangalore torpedoes and then threw them inside the pill boxes killing, everyone inside and rendering the fortifications useless. It was getting dark when the battle was over and we took our objective, but we didn't last long in there as the enemy launched a strong counterattack. Instead of meeting them (the counterattack), we withdrew to our original positions.

When the battle began our company "C" consisted of 135-140 men, and when we returned to our original positions we were told that only 20 men were left! It was decided to adopt a "buddy system" for the night; that was two men to a slit trench. This was to avoid the enemy sneaking up on us and slitting our throats if we happened to be alone and fell asleep. The two-man system to a trench was to avoid that, because in such conditions it was expected that at least one would be awake. However, under these circumstances, there was no possibility of sleep. The artillery on both sides sporadically maintained an all-night duel. The dreaded mortars fired on us intermittently throughout the night and the riflemen from both sides shot at each other because sometimes, by watching each other, we saw images. Sometimes we thought that the enemy was coming after us. We saw imaginary objects or enemy soldiers, and we fired at them. The enemy returned the fire to the flash of our rifles and vice-versa. I asked the man who was with me to lay down and try to sleep if he could. This man was an American of Polish descent. He did try, and he laid between my legs in the slit trench we shared and attempted to sleep. At daybreak the fire intensified.

Suddenly I felt as if somebody stuck a red hot dagger on my back. It was very painful. I told my partner, "I think I have been hit."

"Oh, no." he said. "Relax."

I have stated that my partner was lying between my legs. I was on my knees, my elbows resting in the parapet with me holding my M-l rifle in my hands. When I felt the impact of the shrapnel I had difficulty in breathing. I leaned back seeking relief; I was gasping for breath. Then I leaned forward and coughed a mouthful of blood on my partner. He realized that I was hit. He scrambled out of the position he was in and started yelling "Medics! Medics!"

At the same time, he was cutting my clothes with his trench knife. I could feel my blood coming out of the wound, first warm and sticky, then cold. The medics arrived quickly, placed me on a litter and took me to a waiting jeep. They had to take me through a devastating enemy artillery and mortar fire and, naturally, they were scared to death; but me, I was oblivious to all that was taking place. I had difficulty in breathing, therefore, I was moving a lot on the litter, making it difficult for them to carry me.

One of the four said: "Be still, you S.O.B." He was so scared! And one other more calm lit a cigarette and put it in my mouth, thinking that he was doing me a favor. I had a hard time to spit it out because the smoke was making it more difficult to breathe.

When we reached the jeep they fastened the litter to a rig equipped for this purpose, and I was taken to a First Aid Station. When the crew released the litter from the jeep, I recognized one man among them. It was the Argentinean who, when I was placed in a tent, stayed with me, talking to me in Spanish. I don't think I knew what he was saying because of my condition.

Soon a doctor came, worked on me for a little while, and gave me a shot that knocked me completely out. It was a blessing. From there I was taken to Strasburg where the shrapnel was removed from my chest. I was told that the shrapnel was an inch and a quarter and with it splinters of my bone were spread in my lung, which resulted in serious complications. My wife was notified that I was critically wounded and, by mistake, I was listed as "Dead in Action" in the *Oregonian,* a Portland, Oregon newspaper. Luckily, my wife did not see it because her sister Anita hid the paper from Aurora.

29
Hospital Incident in Strasbourg

I was not kept very long in Strasburg. I do remember a few incidents while there, however. After regaining consciousness, the doctor who removed the shrapnel came to see me. He had a bottle of beer in his hand. He asked some questions like "How are you feeling." etc. Then he offered me his beer. His ration of beer was only two or three mottles a week and he shared it with his patients!

"This is good for you." he said, and insisted in my having what was left of the bottle. Even though I was not a beer drinker (because I got awfully sick drinking too much of it when I was 13 years old), I drank it.

On this ward there were seven wounded men. One was a German who was cared for the same as we were, which is a credit to our people. However, there was one problem. The shortage of Penicillin. A heated argument developed among the G.I.s, some in favor of administering Penicillin to him, others against it. I did not participate in the debate for I was too weak. I never knew the outcome of the debate. I, along with many other wounded G.I.s was taken to a huge warehouse on Christmas Eve. The place was incredible. It was a smoke-filled huge building and literally hundreds of G.I.s were on litters on the floor, waiting to be loaded onto the hospital train the following day to be taken to various general hospitals in France. The wait in this warehouse on Christmas Eve was terrible.

It was almost impossible to breathe because of the smoke generated by the large number of G.I.s smoking. Those who were not too badly wounded smoked, talked loudly and sang Christmas carols happily, giving the place an atmosphere that is impossible for me to describe. Yet, it was very tough for those men who were seriously and critically wounded who had difficulty in breathing, as well as suffering excruciating pain.

On Christmas of 1944 we were loaded on a hospital train that took us to a city named Miracourt. On our way to this place our train, which I am sure was clearly marked with big red crosses on top of the cars, was unmercifully attacked by the German planes. The train was strafed by the enemy. I don't know whether they inflicted any casualties, but I do know that they knocked out our train's heating system. It got so cold on the train that the personnel placed between seven or nine blankets on me.

At the general hospital in Miracourt, I was taken, by mistake, to the wrong ward. The wards in the hospitals were efficiently arranged. Those with chest injuries, amputees, etc. I was a chest case, but I was taken to the amputees' ward. I was failing fast. The chief doctor of this ward realized it and asked the doctors who were chest specialists to examine me, which they did. Two of the doctors (we addressed them as majors rather than doctors), Drs. Bruer and Burbank, came to see me one evening and suggested that I be transferred to their ward, which I was a couple of days later. I was placed in an aisle on a cot because there were no more hospital beds available. It was very uncomfortable.

I think that some little incidents that happened during my long stay in this hospital may be of interest to the reader. When the man closest to me on my left died, his body was taken out, the bed was changed, and I was placed in it. It had some sort of psychological effect on me. I thought I might be the next to die in that bed.

After my first operation in this hospital I did not improve, so the doctors decided that I needed another operation. One night Dr. Bruer came to see me as he and Dr. Burbank often did. This time Dr. Bruer came alone, sat on the edge of my bed and told me diplomatically that I needed to be operated on again and the reasons for it.

Kashpar after he recovered from the war injuries.

He told me that my right lung was completely collapsed and in order to reinflate it they needed to perform an operation. I protested, saying that I was feeling fine, that I had no pain, and that I'd rather not have any more operations. After a long discussion, I told him that he was the doctor and whatever he thought best for me I would go along with. The following morning (February 2, 1945), they performed the operation, and from then on I was slowly, but surely improving.

The strangest thing about this operation that I remember was that the morning of the operation while waiting in the operating room I could hear the doctors and nurses talking, but since I was semi-conscious I did not know what they were saying except someone on the team said: "O.K. let's go to work," or "Let's go at it," or something to that effect. I sort of felt them surrounding me and pretty soon I felt like somebody slapped something on my face. It was chloroform. I tried to fight it, but couldn't, and the strange thing was that as I was going under I "saw" myself walking hand in hand with my son, him holding my hand with one hand and beating a drum with the other hand! Then I went under completely.

My recovery was a lengthy one. I would like to relate some anecdotes that transpired during it. From the moment my shrapnel was removed I was getting a shot of penicillin every three hours, twenty-four hours a day for approximately sixty days. One night a medic came to administer the ritual shot. He goofed. When he tried to pull the needle out, the part that contained the medicine disconnected from the needle and spread the penicillin all over my face. I cussed him badly, but he was such a nice guy he said to me, unperturbed: "Relax, Mac, I didn't mean to do that and I am sorry." Then he gave me another shot.

The "ward boys" of the hospital were German prisoners. They were very efficient men. I became acquainted with the one who took care of my needs. He was known as "Fritz." That was not his real name, but like the G.I.s were known as either Joe or Mac, the Germans were own as either Fritz or Heinz. This particular prisoner was known as Fritz and he answered to that name.

After my last operation I was almost paralyzed on my bed for a long time. One night after I was allowed to drink water, I called for the ward boy asking for water. Fritz came and decided to bring me fresh water. He placed the canteen in my mouth, left hand on the canteen, and then held my hand knowing that after I was through drinking I would give an indication that I had enough. Because of this kind of thing, we developed a very good friendship. Whenever he could he came to see me, and sat on the edge of my bed to chat. When he was transferred to a different unit I did not get to see him for sometime. One day I spotted him with other prisoners. He was in a unit that transported the wounded G.I.s to hospital trains or wherever they needed to be transferred. I went to talk to him. He did not recognize me at first, because I had improved so much during the two months or so that he was away. We shook hands and talked a little bit. I am sure that he was genuinely happy to see that I was doing so good. I went to my bed, picked up a carton of cigarettes and a half dozen candy bars, and gave them to him. He was so happy that he had tears in his eyes. So did I. We were not allowed to fraternize with the enemy, but there were no laws or forces in the world that legislate that kind of law. We became friends and nothing could stop that.

There was one nurse in our ward whose duty was to give hypos to the G.I.s to put us to sleep. I used to beg her to give me a hypo, but she always ignored me. It was because she couldn't inject the shot whenever someone asked her for it, only at certain intervals. She also assisted Dr. Bruer on his checkups on the patients. One day she and Dt. Bruer stopped by my bed. Those of us who were getting Penicillin shots had a red ribbon laced at the foot of out beds and on this particular checkup Dr. Bruer ordered the penicillin for me be discontinued and the ribbon removed from my bed.

The next day when the doctor came along with the nurse on his routine checkup he said, "I thought I ordered that ribbon be removed."

The nurse got worried because she didn't remove it for orneriness. I said "That is right, doctor, but I forgot to tell the nurse."

"Well, let's remove it right now," he said, and the nurse did so. Because of the ribbon being there an extra twenty-four hours, I was given at least seven extra shots.

After they completed their rounds the nurse came to see me and apologized for what she did. "I thought you were a crabby old . . . " she said, "but you are a good sport." She said that she was sorry for what she had done, ruffled my hair, and asked me "Are we friends?"

"We sure are." I replied

I also told her that I had given her the impression of being crabby but it was not because of my desire to harass her, but because she was the one who administered the pain killer I needed or wanted so bad.

From Miracourt I was taken to Marseille, and after a

lengthy recovery period, I was sent home.

I said earlier that the Americans, as good soldiers and tough fighters they were, they lacked discipline. That is the wrong way to put it. I shouldn't have said "they." I should have said "we Americans" for I am one of "they." In the course of this narrative, I am sure that the reader has noticed that I described some men that I was with as American of Polish descent, American of Filipino descent, American of Italian descent, American of Greek descent, American of Jewish descent, etc. So why should I say "them" or "they" when I too am an American of Basque descent? In the few remaining pages, when referring to "Americans" I will use the pronoun "we or us." Because I am proud to be one. Now, we Americans that lack in discipline as I have stated before, which to me is a virtue rather than vice, make up for it in sense of humor, which to me is a virtue. For example: In this hospital in Miracourt the G.I.'s who needed certain items for their necessities, they called for the ward boys and our calls went like this:

"Fritz, I need a P.38!" P. 38 was a very popular airplane, a double fuselage fighter, one of the fastest planes, perhaps the fastest of all nations involved in the W.W.II and our G.I.'s named the urinals after it!

And then someone hollered:

"Heinz, I need a 'flying fortress,'" and we see another German prisoner going by with a bed pan! It was named after our flying fortress which I think were the B-29 bombers.

Another example of American humor: Soon after we captured Bitsweiler, a huge number of prisoners were herded to wherever the prisoners were kept. They were marching at "attention" as they always did and singing their popular song "Lilly Marlene." We made way for them, going to the sidewalks on both sides of the street. Pretty soon some G.I. spotted a short, dark German prisoner, he pointed his finger at him and yelled:

"Look, Superman."

Everybody laughed and yelled Superman! Then some other G.I. placed his left index finger between his nose and his upper lip imitating Hitler's mustache, and, looking at the prisoners, gave the Nazi salute yelling:

"Heil Hitler, just in case we lose."

30
Return Home

Three hundred wounded G.I.s were loaded on the American ship, S.S. Mariposa, in the port of Marseille, France, bound for home. But first the ship, with us aboard, had to go to Naples, Italy, to pick up a large number of our Air Force people, our "Glamour Boys," who were eligible for discharge on the point system, which was the method our government adopted to discharge those who served the longest in the service.

After three days in Naples the ship left for the U.S.A. The facilities on the ship were very good. The wounded soldiers had sort of separate quarters from the others. It was not a hospital ship. It was a cruiser.

On May 8, 1945 we crossed the strait of Gibraltar. Soon after we entered the Atlantic Ocean we got the news over the loud speaker that the war in Europe was over. Everybody let out a loud yell of approval. Suddenly, everybody started to think and worry about the German U-boats. What if they didn't know the war was over and attacked us? But that feat was dispelled soon when we were told that because of our ship's speed the U-boats had no chance of harming it. I wasn't sure whether we were going to the U.S.A. or England and it worried me because I thought that perhaps we might end up in some English hospital. A couple of days after going through Gibraltar I knew that we were heading home because we were traveling straight west.

We were taken to Camp Miles Standish! The same place we sailed from, but the conditions were much better than when we left. In the few days that we were there, we had some sort of entertainment every night put on by "celebrities," but the only one I attended was the show put on by Roy Rogers and his horse Trigger. The reason I remember that show is that there was a rather sad incident. The show was interrupted in the middle of it by an important announcement. The announcement was: "All the men quartered in barracks number . . . report to your quarters." That meant that many of these men were processed and were to be sent home. The men stampeded out of the theater, deserting poor old Roy Rogers and Trigger. Even the men whose barracks number was not announced left the show in case that someone by mistake had omitted mentioning their barracks number. I was one of them. On my way out I passed very close to Roy Rogers. I paused momentarily, and thought that I could detect a genuine expression of sympathy on his face. I thought that he seemed happy to see these men go to be reunited with their loved ones. There was not a sign of egotism about him.

Within a few days I was sent to Madison General Hospital in Tacoma, Washington. There were only nine wounded G.I.s on the train's Pullman coach. It was a very pleasant trip from Boston to Tacoma.

After a few days of processing in Tacoma, I got to go home on a ninety-day convalescent furlough. I was very excited. The closer I got to Boise, the faster my heart beat. About 10:00 p.m. of May 31, 1945 our train arrived in Boise, the same train station that I arrived at eleven years before. The coach in which I was riding stopped about a block from the station, but I was sure that there would be somebody waiting for me this time. It was raining. I stepped out of the train, looked toward the station, and spotted my wife running towards me. When we met I put my duffel bag down and we embraced. She wrapped her arms around my waist, buried her little head on my chest and cried and cried. And there we were like a couple of dummies getting all wet in the rain.

When we separated she gave me a long, close look and exclaimed: "Daddy, you look so much better than I expected! I expected to see you badly mutilated."

"No, my injuries were internal," but I don't think she even heard me.

"Come, let's go see our son," she said as she took hold of my hand and led me into the station.

I picked my duffel bag up and went with her into the station where my wife's sister and her husband were waiting for us. They took us to their home where my wife and son were staying for a few days in anticipation of my homecoming. There I saw my son for the first time. Alfred Joseph! He was sleeping on his tummy so I couldn't see his face, but I knew that he was a cute little guy. He had thick, bushy, black hair, and I wanted to pick him up or at least touch him, but I didn't dare, fearing that I might disturb him.

Aurora, my wife, said "Go ahead, pick him up." or "Touch him."

But I didn't want to wake him up. That wasn't necessary, because he soon started to cry. I picked him up, but he struggled to free himself from me. He wanted his mom. He didn't like me for he felt that I was an intruder. Mom belonged to him and I had no business there. But it did not last long as we soon became friends. After a few days in Boise the three of us went to Jordan Valley, Oregon to spend my convalescent furlough. Alfred Joseph was 1 1 months old when I first had seen him.

31
My Recovery

During that time I spent three weeks at Gowen Field Air Force Base Hospital in Boise, and at the end of ninety days I had to report back to Fort Lewis, Washington, and wait to see whether I was going to recover fully from my injuries and be sent to the Pacific Theater of War or be discharged. While awaiting the results we were given the opportunity to attend some classes in the schools that were set up in the camp. I enrolled in two of them and took one subject in each, one in agriculture, because I always wanted to be a farmer and wanted to learn to drive a tractor. The other subject I chose was English, because I had the desire to improve mine. This class didn't last long because, according to the lady teacher, I wasn't saying anything right, grammatically or otherwise, and my pronunciation was very bad according to her. I quit and became a number in the statistics of "drop outs" after about two weeks of school. As a corporal, buck sergeant, staff sergeant, section leader and acting platoon sergeant, I did not have any difficulty issuing the necessary orders or the soldiers to understand me. I think that the problem with her was that she couldn't tell the difference between the grammatical aspects of English and the foreigner's accent, so I quit.

In about two months of waiting I was ordered to go before the medical board for a medical evaluation. This was the board that determined whether we were going to be discharged, the rate of disability that would be assigned, or whether we would be kept in the Armed Services for future needs or conflicts.

Kashpar after the war.

Several days after my appearance before the board I was summoned to the headquarters and was notified that the board's decision was to give me a medical discharge and the board set the rate of my disability at 100%, temporarily. Giving me the discharge was good news, and I was happy to be going back to my wife and son, but the 100% disability bit was disturbing. In a few days I was discharged and came home for good. Once again, for the third time in eleven years, I wound up in the same depot and for the second time my wife was waiting for me. This was my permanent homecoming. A few days after my arrival I wanted to start working, even though I was 100% disabled. After days of pounding the Boise streets looking for a job I did find one with a trucking company, but after a month working there I realized that I couldn't handle it. One evening I went to the place of work and found the manager working late. I told him that I was having difficulty with my job, that I was not producing what I should and that I was resigning. "I am glad that you decided to resign because I was planning on firing you." he said. That is gratitude, I thought!

I thought he could have offered me something that was not as strenuous as working on the dock handling merchandise. This man was younger than I, but somehow he stayed home during the war, making a lot of money. After that I didn't look for any job because I realized that I was not able to do too much because of my physical limitations. In two or three months my family and I went to visit our friends, the Egurrola family who farmed in Homedale, Idaho. The head of the family, Joe Egurrola, was one of the nicest and most generous men I had ever known. Through him I found a job working at a labor camp in Homedale as an interpreter between the farmers and Mexican workers. These workers were from Mexico and spoke no English and the farmers who employed them did not speak Spanish, so even though my English was somewhat shaky, I was a help to both parties. My job was temporary, only for six months during the farming season, but I lasted twenty-three years with the association. These men, the board of directors of that association, consisted of five men of which four were veterans of WWI. All five of them, as well as the members of the labor association, were so good to me in contrast to the man in Boise who told me that "... he was going to fire me."

While in Homedale, we had another child, a boy whom we named Roy.

I was involved in many things while in Homedale. I was elected the Commander of the American Legion and even though I knew nothing about the Boy Scouts, I became a scout master for about four years. When I was asked to run for city council, I thought that whenever a request of this kind was made of me

I was supposed to do it as a citizen's obligation, and because of that belief I ran against two other men hoping that I would be defeated. But no, I beat them both and served one term as a councilman.

At the end of my term the elections were coming up and I was approached by a group of men suggesting that I should run for mayor. No way! I wouldn't run for mayor. I had no political aspirations and besides, I felt that I had fulfilled my obligation as a citizen.

"Well," the spokesman of the group said, "Think about it. Sleep on it."

Several days later I had a call from the city clerk telling me that there were some petitions waiting for my signature for my approval. "What petitions?" I asked her.

"These petitions are asking you to run for mayor." She said.

I didn't want to do that, and I wasn't going to do it. I was worried, so I decided to call our city attorney telling him about the situation and my feelings about not wanting to run for mayor. The attorney, my good friend Dick Eismann, laughed. Whenever I talked to him and if he detected a sign of excitement on my part he laughed. I told him that according to the city clerk there was in the neighborhood of two hundred signatures on the petition. Eismann told me after he was through laughing that there was no law in Idaho that said I had to sign the document, but if I didn't it would be like telling all the people who wanted me to run for mayor to "go to hell."

"So, Kashpar, you have two options, either sign it or tell your friends to go to . . . you know."

I talked with my wife about it and decided to sign it, to become a candidate in the hope that I would be defeated. But no, again I won the election and served one term as a mayor and became a big fish in a little pond.

About the time that my term as mayor expired, a delegation consisting of two men, State Senator Arley Parkins, Democrat from Owyhee County, and Everett Colley, publisher of the *Owyhee Chronicle,* came to our house in Homedale and asked me to run for senator from Owyhee County. Senator Parkins was retiring and was looking for someone to run in his place and these two men thought I was the man that could be elected as a Democrat in the staunch Republican county. I declined to run because I felt that I couldn't be an effective legislator for the following reasons; Idaho's Legislature at that time was composed of two groups; one of lawyers, the majority of whom were employed by big corporations and as such could devote all their time to devising ideas or projects that would be beneficial to the corporations who employed them (these were the "City Slickers"); the second group consisted mostly of well-to-do retired ranchers and farmers. This group was known as "Cowboys." Each of these groups had all the time they needed to devote to governmental affairs. I, as a manager of a labor camp, didn't have the needed time to devote to the legislation.

32
Life in my Beloved Idaho

Our life as a family while our boys were growing up was very happy for several years. During these years I had many interesting encounters. I lost all contact with the land of my ancestors during WW II. I was sure that during the war the Basques became extinct because in spite of the fact that the Fascist axis was destroyed the Fascist regime of Francisco Franco was allowed to remain in power in Spain in spite of the tremendous help Fascist Spain gave to the German-Italian axis war effort by allowing the use of the Canary Islands as the main base of operations for the German U-boats blockade of the Atlantic where thousands of Americans were killed and untold numbers of tons of war materials was lost as the result of it. While in Homedale we had another son whom we named Roy. He was seven and a half years Al's junior.

One day I went to the post office after my mail and found a magazine addressed to someone else in our P.O. Box. The magazine came from Mexico and its name was "Euzko Deya" (The Voice of the Basque). I went to the counter with it and told the clerk that I did not know this man and asked her what she was going to do with the magazine. She replied that since there was no return guarantee it will be disposed of in some way.

"Why?" she asked me.

"Because I would like to have it and if I knew where you will throw it I would pick it up." I answered. "Well, here" she said, "take it."

I did take it with me and through it and subsequent issues I received, for I subscribed to it immediately, I was informed of what was going on in the Basque Country. I developed a lot of contacts throughout Mexico and South America, but not much in the Basque Country because of Franco's oppressive regime's strict censorship, but mostly through the Basque refugees in South and Central America I learned that they were far from being extinct as I thought they may be. They were fighting just as tenaciously for their freedom and for their right to exist as they fought against the first invaders, the Iberians, over 3000 years B.C. (The Basque situation is analogous with that of the Jews.)

In the meantime a group of young Americans of Basque descent organized a group of Basque dancers known as the "Oinkari" = "Oin" (foot) and "-kari" (suffix that denotes object-matter as in: "sendatu" (to cure) and "sendakari" (doctor M.D. "He-she who cures.)" The same applies to "Oinkari" literally meaning those who perform with their feet. This group of young dancers performed throughout the U.S. representing Idaho in New York, Washington D.C. Rotunda, Seattle, Washington World's Fair, and other places and often were asked who were the Basques and they couldn't answer very well. These youngsters' grandparents did not have the chance to learn Basque history because the Spanish authorities wouldn't allow it so they couldn't pass it on to their children, but they did teach the Basque language to their children in the U.S.A. who in turn their children failed to teach it to their offspring, which I am guilty of too. So, when away from home in New York or wherever and a member of the Oinkari was asked to say a few words in Basque, they couldn't. They found this situation somewhat awkward, so they decided that they should learn some Basque. A delegation of young Oinkari dancers came to our home in Homedale and asked me if I would teach them some Basque and I accepted the challenge. How I was going to teach them I did not know for I had no experience in reaching and what is more, there was no material to teach it with. One day while visiting my friend and our parish priest, Father George Brennan, an Irish émigré, we touched on the subject of my predicament, namely my lack of knowledge to teach as well as the lack of materials to teach Basque. He said, "Perhaps I could help you."

"How," I asked him.

"Just a minute. I will be right back," and he left the room and a minute later he returned. "Here," he said, handing a book to me. "This book may help you," he said.

It was a Basque grammar! The first one I had ever seen in my life. Since the speaking of our native language, Basque, was prohibited in Euzkadi-Basque Country material related to anything Basque was also prohibited by the rulers of Spain, particularly during the period of Primo de Rivera's dictatorship. Therefore, I had never seen a Basque grammar during the years I was growing up in the Basque Country. Yet, this priest from Ireland in one of his visits to the Iberian Peninsula found a grammar book that survived the civil guards (civil!), raids and confiscation, bought it (smuggled it is more appropriate) to Idaho and loaned it to me for the purpose I needed it with the admonition that 'You can use it for as long as you need, but when you are through with it, I want it back."

And so, with the help of this grammar book, we started our Basque language classes, and with the notes that I saved in preparation for the lessons I developed a method to learn Basque. A Basque scholar, refugee of the Spanish Civil War (1936-39) lived and worked in New York for an American Oil Co. was transferred to Colombia S.A. as the manager of the oil company operation in South America. He was multilingual and as such contributed many articles and essays to many American publications. Also, this man, whose name was Francisco Abrisqueta, developed a personal library which at the time he donated it to Harvard University was valued in the neighborhood of $250,000. Mr. Arbrisqueta reviewed the method I had developed and published the review in the "Boletin de Estudios Bascos de America," published in Buenos Aires, Argentina and distributed all throughout Latin America, and in the U.S.A.

Risking of being accused of vanity I wish to include some excerpts of his review: "Euzkera Itzketan zelan ikasi = How to learn to speak Basque." (This is my translation to English from Spanish): After the outline of Basque Grammar by W.J. Van Eys published in London in 1883 as a part of the Trübner's Collection of Simplified Grammars of the principal Asiatic and European Languages I believe that the *Introduction to Basque* as the author calls his work with modesty is the second method in Basque-English that had ever been published to date.

"Several years ago, a group of young North American Basque Americans knowing my desires to maintain the Basque language and culture" says Kashpar in his wonderful manuscript "they asked me if I would accept the direction of a course in Basque. It was a tough challenge to me because until that time I never had any experience in teaching. However, in view of the fact that these young people's interest in learning the language was so sincere, I did not want to discourage them. As a consequence, 57 avid students and a somewhat insecure 'professor' gathered in Boise, Idaho on the 10th of September, 1963 to initiate perhaps the first class of Basque to ever be taught in the U.S.A."

About the same time that this method came into existence, one of the Western U.S.A. universities initiated a Basque Studies program, part of which was to offer the learning of the Basque language. The director of the institution became aware of the method and asked me if I would send them a copy of the manuscript for their examination and possibly for the publication of it through their institution's press. But the committee of experts who reviewed it came to the conclusion that it was inadequate for their purposes which was to teach Basque.

They proceeded to teach Basque to the English speaking students using a Spanish method "temporarily" until the said institution of higher education could develop a more adequate method. Twenty years later, the experts have not developed anything not only comparable but nothing to compare it with our simple method reviewed by Mr. Abrisqueta.

My wife's mother was Mercedes. I'll call her Mertxe. She was one of the first Basque pioneers who emigrated to Idaho in the early 1900's. She married a man by the name of Simon Akordagoitia in Jordan Valley, Oregon, and they bought a ranch in a place known as Birch Creek located at the backwaters of the Owyhee Reservoir. There they ran about six to eight thousand head of sheep using this ranch as their headquarters for their stock raising operation. As she grew older, two of her three daughters took turns taking care of her as she was a widow and living alone. When she was with my wife, Aurora and me, we

Possibly the first Basque class ever in Idaho. September 10, 1963.

talked a lot about their early life in America.

Some of the incidents that took place during the time these pioneers were raising their families and making a living in the most remote areas of Idaho and eastern Oregon are worth repeating. I would like to share some of these with the readers of this book.

From the top of the plateau to their house was a distance of about three miles of a very steep slope. The house was located about three "blocks" from the Owyhee River so deep in the canyon that no sun was visible in the winter even on very clear days. Every so often the family went to Jordan Valley to buy groceries. It took a day to drive the wagon to Jordan Valley and another day to return to the ranch. On one of these trips as the family which consisted of Mertxe, Simon and four children at that time were returning home from Jordan Valley, a rattlesnake spooked the horses between the plateau and the canyon where their home was. The horses ran away down the canyon as fast as they could. Simon couldn't stop them, and Mertxe realizing that he couldn't stop them decided to do something to prevent the almost certain death or serious injuries, got hold of the oldest child, a boy, and threw him out of the wagon trying to land him on the biggest bush to break the fall; then the second child, a girl; then she took the two littlest ones—one in each arm—and jumped out of the wagon with them. Soon the wagon and Simon in it were out of her sight. She gathered the children, which was not hard because of their crying and calling for their Amatxu (dear Mother). She picked up the youngest one in her arms (who 20 years later became my wife), and with the rest of them holding her hand or skirt trailed down the canyon towards their house. As they advanced towards their house, Mertxe could see parts of their groceries such as flour, sugar, etc. scattered all over. Soon she spotted Simon coming towards them, and as they met he asked, "Everybody o.k.?" "Yes," said Mertxe, "we are scared, but not hurt. What about you?" "I am fine," he said, "I just couldn't stop them, but I am not hurt." So all of them proceeded towards their home on foot. When they reached the house, the horses were by the gate of the corral with only the tongue of the wagon attached to the harness. The rest of the wagon, along with the groceries were gone. The horses were standing sweaty, nervous and foaming at their mouths. Simon, too, realizing the futility of trying to stop the horses had jumped from the wagon and let them go.

I would also like to share another story that I think is a typical scene of the American West where Mertxe and her four little children were the main protagonists.

One morning, around noon, Mertxe spotted a man on horseback approaching the ranch house. She watched him as he came closer and began to worry about him. He was a typical cowboy complete with guns slung from each side. When he reached the house, he dismounted and Mertxe stood waiting at the porch door. They exchanged some greetings, the man in English and Mertxe in Basque for she did not know English. By sign language, she had him come in and pumped some water in the wash basin for him to wash his hands and gave him a clean towel to dry on, and went to the kitchen to fix something for him to eat. After he was through washing, she indicated by sign language for him to sit down and eat the hearty meal she had prepared. Hospitality was an unwritten law.

The children, four of them at the time, ranging from eight to two years, bunched up in a corner wide-eyed and scared watching the stranger. The man spoke to them, but they never answered him for they couldn't speak English either. Whatever Mertxe served him, he ate as fast as he could and got up just as soon as he finished eating, and with a very formal and polite farewell, he left. The only thing Mertxe understood from what he said was, "Thank you, Maam!" He mounted his horse and left. The mother and the children were all relieved, but not for long for in less than half an hour a group of six or eight men armed to the teeth were coming at a fast pace towards the house. The mother holding her children, who were wrapped around her holding her skirt apron or whatever, met the group of men 3y the door of the porch. The men did not dismount. One of them with a badge asked her some questions that she couldn't answer because if the language barrier. However, by sign language and some broken English she made them understand that there was a man in her place that she had fed and that he then left, "aruntz juan da" which in Basque means, "he went that way." The leader of the group thanked her and they left in the direction she had indicated with her hand.

In 1968 my wife became ill. After extensive testing, the diagnosis was that she had cancer. It was devastating to all of us! The next three years were very difficult and through series of operations she was mutilated, and for more than three years she was in constant pain. On November of 1971 she, like the Spaniards say, "Delivered her soul to God," while I was holding her little head in my hands. I closed her mouth and shut her eyes, and when the doctor came in and made it official that she was gone I went outside, and contrary to a Spanish song that says, "Un hombre macho no debe llorar" which means that a "macho" man shouldn't cry, I did cry. I waited until her body was taken to the mortuary, went home and notified my sons and relatives. The older son came to our house, but the younger one was at the University of Idaho and it was not possible for him to come that night. Aurora was gone! She was a relatively young woman when she died, 53 years old. I was with her continuously in the hospital. About an hour before she died I was with her, alone, in the hospital room.

She said "Daddy, I want to talk to you. I am going to be gone pretty soon and—I interrupted her—"No, honey, don't talk like that."

"Daddy," she started again, "please don't interrupt me. I want to tell you something."

"O.K.," I said, "I won't interrupt you."

She spoke falteringly, gasping for breath, "I am going now, and when I go I don't want you to be fretting, crying or feeling sorry for yourself. Life is for the living. It is my turn now. Someday you will come to where I am going now. One thing I want you to do is to find yourself a good woman who will take care of you because if you don't the filth will eat you up because you don't know how to take care of yourself.

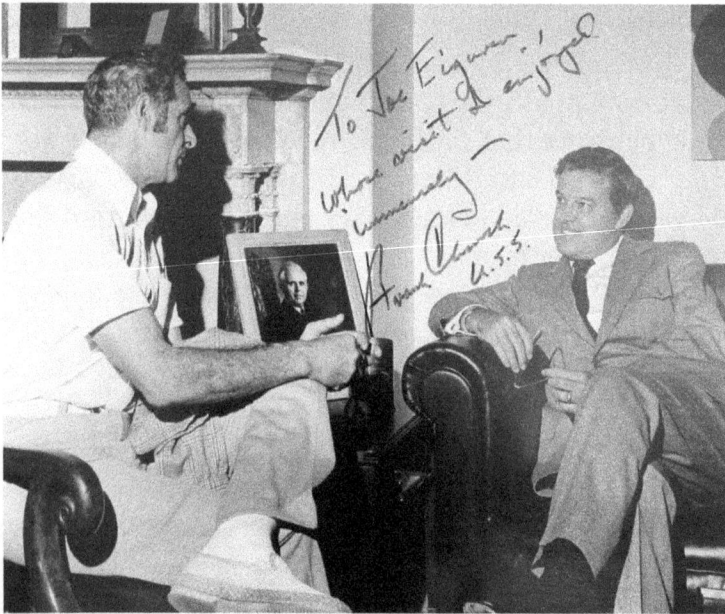

Kashpar with Senator from Idaho Frank Church ca. 1975.

You can't cook, you don't know how to wash your clothes, you don't know how to do anything."

In spite of the seriousness of the situation, and even realizing the imminence of her approaching death, she was more concerned about my future and well being. She was concerned about my inability to take care of myself.

About three years prior to her sickness, I changed jobs. I resigned my job with the farmers association and went to work for the Idaho State Department of Employment in Nampa, Idaho, and we moved from Homedale to be closer to Nampa. After Aurora's death I moved to Boise and lived alone, except when my son Roy came home from college.

While working for the Department, I had an opportunity to go to Euzkadi (Basque Country) to teach Basque history and language on the staff of Boise State University, so I took a leave of absence for nine months and taught and resided in a college only twenty-five kilometers from the town where I grew up.

Kashpar with Senator from Idaho James A. McClure ca. 1985.

Upon my return to the United States, I went back to work at the employment service and resumed my normal life.

A year later, tragedy struck again. Our older son, Alfred, was killed in an automobile accident on August 26, 1976. He was only 32 years old with a beautiful future ahead of him. Of all the tragedies that occurred in our lives, the death of our son had the most devastating effect on me. I stated before at the beginning of this narrative that after the death of my father our life was a continuous struggle to survive. Now I thought, why struggle? To be rewarded with the unnecessary death of a beautiful, gentle, talented young man with so much compassion for humanity? After his death, people came to see me and told me that this was God's plan. I was not supposed to question God's plan! They held my hands and prayed. What a bunch of nonsense, I thought. I truly lost all my faith in God. If I dwell on this subject I will get too involved. Perhaps what changed my attitude was a conversation with my son Roy. Because of this tragic event, I had become very depressed, and perhaps I developed suicidal inclinations. One time talking to Roy about my feelings, I told him that I didn't care whether I lived or not, and in fact I would just as soon be dead.

The poor kid said, "What about me, Dad? My mother and my brother are gone. You are the only one I have left, and if you leave me, then what?"

That affected me deeply.

Among the people I met in my place of employment was one lady, the receptionist, whose name was Jean. At a farewell party given for one of the staff who was leaving, Jean and my wife met and established a warm friendship between the two. During the last several months that Aurora's health was rapidly deteriorating, Jean visited her often, almost every weekend. Whenever Jean visited she always brought something, soup, pie, etc. and helped Aurora with her hair. She looked forward to Jean's visits.

Sometime after Aurora's death, Jean and I started attending concerts, dining out together and attending churches, hers and mine, from time to time. Just a little over a year after Al's death, Jean and I were married on November 19, 1977 in Seattle in a very simple ceremony with her sister and my son, Roy, as attendants. In Jean I found what Aurora wished for me, a woman who cared for me, and the feeling was mutual. We settled into a normal life. Jean has been on crutches as the result of polio ever since she was a very young woman, and everybody who sees her walking with churches thinks she is handicapped. Everyone except Jean herself.

After a few years of happy marriage in spite of all of the tragedies that had taken place, tragedy struck again. We received word that a small, two-passenger plane was reported lost between Moscow, Idaho and Boise. There were only two people

Kashpar in Boise ca. 1992.

on the plane, the pilot and a passenger who was Jean's son, David
Marts, from her previous marriage. About 40 planes and helicopters searched the area (organized and coordinated by the Idaho
State Aeronautics Division), but with negative results. To this
day, no sign of the plane or the men have been found yourself.
Life is for the living. It is my turn now. Someday you will come to
where I am going now. One thing I want you to do is to find yourself a good woman who will take care of you because if you don't

the filth will eat you up because you don't know how to take care of yourself. You can't cook, you don't know how to wash your clothes, you don't know how to do anything."

In spite of the seriousness of the situation, and even realizing the imminence of her approaching death, she was more concerned about my future and well being. She was concerned about my inability to take care of myself.

About three years prior to her sickness, I changed jobs. I resigned my job with the farmers association and went to work for the Idaho State Department of Employment in Nampa, Idaho, and we moved from Homedale to be closer to Nampa. After Aurora's death I moved to Boise and lived alone, except when my son Roy came home from college.

While working for the Department, I had an opportunity to go to Euzkadi (Basque Country) to teach Basque history and language on the staff of Boise State University, so I took a leave of absence for nine months and taught and resided in a college only twenty-five kilometers from the town where I grew up.

Upon my return to the United States, I went back to work at the employment service and resumed my normal life.
A year later, tragedy struck again. Our older son, Alfred, was killed in an automobile accident on August 26, 1976. He was only 32 years old with a beautiful future ahead of him. Of all the tragedies that occurred in our lives, the death of our son had the most devastating effect on me. I stated before at the beginning of this narrative that after the death of my father our life was a continuous struggle to survive. Now I thought, why struggle?

To be rewarded with the unnecessary death of a beautiful, gentle, talented young man with so much compassion for humanity? After his death, people came to see me and told me that this was God's plan. I was not supposed to question God's plan! They held my hands and prayed. What a bunch of nonsense, I thought. I truly lost all my faith in God. If I dwell on this subject I will get too involved. Perhaps what changed my attitude was a conversation with my son Roy. Because of this tragic event, I had become very depressed, and perhaps I developed suicidal inclinations. One time talking to Roy about my feelings, I told him that I didn't care whether I lived or not, and in fact I would just as soon be dead.

The poor kid said, "What about me, Dad? My mother and my brother are gone. You are the only one I have left, and if you leave me, then what?"

That affected me deeply.

Among the people I met in my place of employment was one lady, the receptionist, whose name was Jean. At a farewell party given for one of the staff who was leaving, Jean and my wife met and established a warm friendship between the two. During the last several months that Aurora's health was rapidly deteriorating, Jean visited her often, almost every weekend. Whenever Jean visited she always brought something, soup, pie, etc. and helped Aurora with her hair. She looked forward to Jean's visits.

Sometime after Aurora's death, Jean and I started attending concerts, dining out together and attending churches, hers and mine, from time to time. Just a little over a year after Al's death, Jean and I were married on November 19, 1977 in Seattle in a very simple ceremony with her sister and my son, Roy, as attendants. In Jean I found what Aurora wished for me, a woman who cared for me, and the feeling was mutual. We settled into a normal life. Jean has been on crutches as the result of polio ever since she was a very young woman, and everybody who sees her walking with crutches thinks she is handicapped. Everyone except Jean herself.

After a few years of happy marriage in spite of all of the tragedies that had taken place, tragedy struck again. We received word that a small, two-passenger plane was reported lost between Moscow, Idaho and Boise. There were only two people on the plane, the pilot and a passenger who was Jean's son, David Marts, from her previous marriage. About forty planes and helicopters searched the area (organized and coordinated by the Idaho State Aeronautics Division), but with negative results. On August 4th 1987 we received word that the remains of Jean's son were found.

We now live a quiet life in the beautiful foothills of Boise close to our remaining children, and grandchildren, five from Jean's side and two from mine.

Epilogue

On August 4th, 1987, we recieved word that the remains of Jean's son were found.

www.ingramcontent.com/pod-product-compliance
Lightning Source LLC
LaVergne TN
LVHW011346080426
835511LV00005B/161